WHAT MEN ARE SAYING ABOUT

THE MAKING OF A DANGEROUS MAN

Ministry Leaders

"I have known Al Larson over the years through the mutual love of Christ, the Navigators, and discipleship through small groups. Al's new *Dangerous Man LifeJournal* is a manual that he was created to write. This book is his 'swan song,' and is filled with ten weeks of masculine centered Bible studies and a prayer journal. This journal is practical and simple to use."

–Dave Wardell PhD
Co-Founder, Promise Keepers, Denver, CO

"Don't even turn the pages of this book unless you want to make some serious progress in becoming the man God wants you to be! Whether young or old, you will find here that Al Larson has skillfully used Scripture and the stories of dangerous men to tap into your deepest longings. I urge you to join with other men and use this tool to help you become the dangerous man you were made to be."

–Mike Jordahl
National Director, The US Collegiate Navigators, Colorado Springs, CO

"*The Making of a Dangerous Man* really hits home for men. Most contemporary authors write books about what men ought to do. Al has written the 'playbook.'"

–Chris Van Brocklin
Director, Evangelical Free Church Association Men's Ministries, Fort Collins, CO

"Most men spend their lives following soul-numbing routines in which one day blends unthinkingly into another—until life is over. This is not what God intended for us and it's a needless waste. Al Larson shows us a pathway out of this trap and into the adventure of engaging daily with God."

–Jim Petersen
Associate to the General Director, The Navigators, Colorado Springs, CO

"In a time when men are crying out for authenticity, Al Larson has given all men a desperately needed guide. Real men are warriors, and warriors are by design very dangerous men. It is time for real men to decide to become real dangerous men and then do more than just talk about it over coffee. For those men waiting for the right study, you now have it."

–Dr. Chuck Stecker
President/Founder, A Chosen Generation, Littleton, CO

"Finally! A study guide that will help men understand what it means to be a man in our society today. This study helps a man to go back to God's blueprint for masculinity: the Bible. There is not a man alive who does not want to be involved in something bigger than himself. This study challenges men regarding who they are and what they are to be about. Every small group of men should go through this."

–Steve Sonderman
Associate Pastor of Men's Ministry, Elmbrook Church, Brookfield, WI

"Al Larson is a man to be listened to and taken seriously. His passion is to equip Christian men on the road from mediocrity to being spiritually dangerous, a threat to the enemy. This journey is not for the faint of heart, but if you are ready for a challenge, this book—practical and inspiring—is for you. Recruit a friend and go for it together."

–Fred Wevodau
Vice President, US Metro Mission, The Navigators, Parker, CO

"If you listed the dangerous men in history, would Jesus Christ make your list? He does if you are Al Larson. Al knows what discipleship is all about. If you are tired of books that tell you how to be a nice guy, pick this one up and you will soon discover how to move from being a disciple of Christ to being dangerous for him."

–Dale L. Eudy
Senior Associate Pastor, Fellowship Community Church, Centennial, CO

"Jesus is the master story teller, painting pictures in men's minds, leading people to action. *Dangerous Man* follows hard in Jesus' path as Al Larson weaves stories of men, who have impacted his life personally, with vivid accounts of other influential men who became dangerous men on earth for the kingdom of God. Together with these stories are relevant portions from the Word of God that provide the content for the Holy Spirit to bring life-changing opportunities to transform us. Here is a process to help us become what we were meant to become!"

–Kim Gustafson
President, Common Ground Consultants, Inc., Hopkins, MN

"This is an inspiring, challenging study! Every man is invited to live dangerously for God by seeing who he is by nature and who he is by God's grace. For men who are serious about discipleship and living by faith."

–Pastor Tom Dekker
New Life Community Church, Milwaukee, WI

"Tired of living an ordinary Christian life? If you are looking for guidance from someone who is leading others to redefine what it means to be a godly man, then you have found what you are looking for! Al Larson's *The Making of a Dangerous Man LifeJournal* is a practical guide that will help men rebuild a strong, God centered identity."

–Shan Moyers
Spiritual Development Minister, LifeBridge Christian Church, Longmont, CO

"Al Larson has done a superb job of providing step by step help from some of the most influential Christians of our age. I highly recommend *The Making of a Dangerous Man* study to every growing Christian and every leader who is helping others to become mature."

–Jim Downing
The Navigators, Colorado Springs, CO

"Al Larson has put together a challenging discipleship course for men. It will set Christian men on the great life adventure of discovering who they are and what God has called them to be and do."

–Dr. Neil T. Anderson
President, Discipleship Counseling Ministries, Franklin, TN
Founder, Freedom in Christ Ministries

"*Dangerous Man* is packed full of motivating and challenging examples of men who weren't willing to settle for mediocrity. You will love the stories and the devotional guide to help you become all that God wants you to be. You can be a major difference maker in the kingdom of God as you grow through this tool."

–Dennis Blevins
Church Discipleship Ministry National Trainer, The Navigators, Gladstone, OR

"*The Making of a Dangerous Man* is a unique and stimulating approach to disciple-making. Do you really want to be a dangerous man? Then follow Jesus Christ, your Commanding Officer, into the heat and heart of battle. He and His matchless Name is the timeless issue. He alone will enable you to do marvelous exploits. But you will also pay a warrior's price—one or more Purple Hearts."

–Bob Boardman
WWII Decorated Combat Marine, The Navigators, Seattle, WA

"*The Making of a Dangerous Man* is thorough, yet its structure delivers relevant learning to engage men: topical Bible study, powerful stories, excellent applications, and the challenge for all men to become dangerous! This is a must for any man serious about their biblical calling to making heart level disciples in today's superficial culture."

–Joe Komarek
Business and Professionals, The Navigators, Minneapolis, MN

"In *The Making of a Dangerous Man*, Al Larson has used man-sized contemporary stories. They resonate. They meet us where we are today. It is stories like these that have impacted me to follow the Lord."

–Gene Soderberg
International Missions Group, The Navigators, Colorado Springs, CO

"The stories of dangerous men and Bible studies are a great motivation for men to grow and to be men of impact for Christ. We must be risk-takers for Christ. Thanks for such a practical *LifeJournal*."

–Dave Johnson
Church Discipleship Ministry, The Navigators, Stow, OH

"What really resonates with me about *The Making of a Dangerous Man* was not only being dangerous for good, but the different pieces Al uses to create this journal format. Stories, Scripture, questions that precipitate understanding and application, and prayer. This is the recipe for the opening of a man's heart to see who God intends for him to be."

–Doug Van Dyke
Executive Director, Northwest Michigan Jesus Ministry, Traverse City, MI

"*The Making of a Dangerous Man* is an excellent process to challenge men with examples of godly men. This is a real opportunity for men to deepen their relationship with Christ in a life-transforming way."

–Les Milner
Director of Small Groups, Majestic Pines Community Church, Mahtomedi, MN

"We too quickly settle for faithful survival when we have been called to so much more. Al Larson has given us a tool calling us to something more—to dangerous living. Wherever you are in your faith journey, you will find *The Making of a Dangerous Man* helpful, challenging, and encouraging."

–Joe Harvey
Executive Minister, LifeBridge Christian Church, Longmont, CO

"Al Larson gives men a tool that equips them to aggressively move from a cluttered life to a focused life. Ten weeks of connecting to God and reflecting on His work in our lives will make any man truly dangerous."

–Brian Doyle
Director, Vision New England Men's Ministries, West Hartford, CT

Men in the Marketplace

"Deep within our souls, men are drawn to a higher cause and purpose beyond ourselves. It is part of who we are meant to be. In *The Making of a Dangerous Man*, Al Larson captures the essence of moving forward in a life full of adventure that is waiting for each of us."

–Ken Ruettgers
Executive Director, GamesOver.org, Sisters, OR
Former tackle, Green Bay Packers

"Can you imagine what this world would be like if every man used the tools and spiritual weapons given to him by God? *The Making of a Dangerous Man* provides men with those tools and gives examples from which we can pattern our lives. Doing *The Making of a Dangerous Man* taught me that to make an impact I must take risks and follow the path God wants for me. And when I take those steps—even the ones that take me out of my comfort zone, I find God is there."

–Jeff Roehrig
Operations Manager, WRS Infrastructure & Environment, Inc., Fort Collins, CO

"I am a man beginning a new journey. Doing *The Making of a Dangerous Man* has helped me start a new walk with God. Through daily reading the Scriptures and prayer, I've seen God's love for me and how I must journey with Him. The stories and Scriptures help you relate to other men who have struggled with their identity and how God transformed their lives."

–Troy Vincent
Campus Manager, Sun Microsystems, Louisville, CO

"*The Making of a Dangerous Man* is a Bible study, a biography of influential men, a daily devotional, a prayer journal, and most importantly, an encounter with the world's most dangerous man. The ten weeks you spend with this tool will change you. After more than 30 years of discipling men of all ages, Al Larson knows what motivates men; he has motivated me, again."

–Gaylen Nagel
Insurance Agent, Stevens Point, WI

"Every conversation I have with Al reminds me that God hasn't given me the spirit of fear, but rather of love and power and a sound mind. I am glad he's put this in the form of a tool to be wielded by every man who's willing to stand strong in Christ. Being a dangerous man frees you to be the kind of man you have always wanted to be."

-Mark McDowell
National Recruiter, National Write Your Congressman, Longmont, CO

"Al Larson captures in *The Making of a Dangerous Man* the essence of what it means to be dangerous for Jesus Christ. The stories of 'dangerous' men are milestones that point the way to being completely sold out for the cause of Christ. Knowing stories of men like this encourage me to be dangerous."

-Brian Krueger
Owner, Krueger Construction, Lafayette, CO

"What I like about *The Making of a Dangerous Man* is that from the beginning to the end it points you to Christ and to see ourselves in His perfect light, forgiven and free (not as the world views us—only as good as our next win). This frees me from getting stuck in guilt-thinking based on performance, —that is when we are dangerous for Him."

-Tony McGeary
Director of Sourcing, The Thomson Corporation, Minneapolis, MN

"Al challenges men with this work to be all God meant them to be. This can help us experience God's pleasure—and be a danger to the enemy."

-Ken Post
District Court Judge, Michigan

"As I began *The Making of a Dangerous Man*, God immediately challenged me about my need to live 'dangerously' and not in a way I deem to be 'safe.' This can be that intentional process that God will use in your life to make you more like Christ."

-Gary Bolenbaugh
Project Manager, Systems Integration Company, MN

"Doing *The Making of a Dangerous Man* during a time of work transition was timely. It helped me think through the issues of identity and purpose. The format with stories of 'dangerous men' will draw participants into thinking about critical issues."

-Bob Morford
Physical Design Mangater, ST Microelectronics Inc., Longmont, CO

"*The Making of a Dangerous Man* is truly inspirational. Any man that has the desire to make an impact with his family, friends, and within his working career, must work through this game plan. This journey will impact men's walk with Christ."

-Stuart Clark
President, McLane Midwest, Danville, IL

Printed in the United States by Morris Publishing
3212 East Highway 30
Kearney, NE 68847
1-800-650-7888

THE MAKING
OF A
DANGEROUS MAN

DANGEROUS MAN LIFEJOURNAL

THIS LIFEJOURNAL BELONGS TO...

_____

Name

_____

Address

_____

Phone

_____

Email

STORIES OF DANGEROUS MEN AND YOUR STORY...

Dedication

To the men and boys in my family who mean the most to me...

To my son, Scott.

How blessed I am to have a son like you!

I am so proud of you.

To my grandson, Jacob.

May you become a man after God's own heart!

You are in my thoughts and prayers every day.

To my son-in-law, Kevin.

Your heart for God and serving people is shining bright!

To my son-in-law, Mark.

You are truly an Ephesians 3:20 gift to our family!

To my grandson, Oliver.

Your happy smile and joyful spirit
are early indicators of the way I believe you will embrace
Christ as your greatest joy and treasure.

To my cousin, Gene Soderberg.

You have been more like a brother to me than a cousin.

Your modeling Christ to me at an early age
launched me on a life journey of following Christ.

CONTENTS

Foreword by Jerry White
13

Thank You
14

There's Danger Ahead!
15

Weeks 1-2 ➢ Getting Ready
19

Weeks 3-5 ➢ A Dangerous Man is Secure in Christ

Week Three ➢ I am God's Son
27

Week Four ➢ I am Loved by God-Forever and Unconditionally
41

Week Five ➢ I am Accepted and Secure
57

Weeks 6-8 ➢ Getting Ready
71

Weeks 6-8 ➢ A Dangerous Man is Significant in Christ

Week Six ➢ I am God's Workmanship
75

Week Seven ➤ I am God's Co-worker
89

Week Eight ➤ I am the Salt and Light of the World
105

The Most Dangerous Man Who Ever Lived
121

Week 9 ➤ Key Learnings
123

Week 10 ➤ Your Story
126

Prayer Journal
131

Leader's Guide
135

Men on My Team
140

Frequently Asked Questions
143

Notes
147

Foreword
by Jerry E. White

Two of my grandsons are on their school's wrestling team. My sports are handball, fast pitch softball pitching, and volleyball. I knew little of wrestling until these last two years. I watched Jerad and Josh lose almost every match in their first year. But Mary and I, their parents, and their siblings came to almost every match and cheered them on. Their dad had been a wrestler and knew what they were going through. Finally, they each posted a win—then several wins. Not having wrestled myself, I had to learn the judging and scoring. It is a sport where no one can help the individual wrestler. He is totally on his own. Three, two-minute periods of grappling, sweat, and strain comprise each match.

Recently, I was helped in my view of the sport at a character symposium at the Air Force Academy where Kyle Maynard spoke. He was one of the top ten Georgia high school wrestlers. He was born with no arms or legs, just stubs for appendages. He said of wrestling, "The first two minutes require skill. The second two minutes require strength. The third two minutes require heart." This is a great lesson on how to live in the daily battles of life.

The Making of a Dangerous Man requires all three-in full measure. Of the three, heart is imperative. It is what keeps a man going when there is nothing else left. But you will not get to that third period when heart is needed unless you have mastered skill and developed strength. In the midst of each period, we need the encouragement of others, regardless of how well we are doing.

The enemy (Satan and his kingdom) will encounter no danger from a man who thinks he can survive with good intentions and sincerity. Any man who thinks he can survive as a believer without understanding the key life issues he will face, and without developing the skills and strength necessary for the battle, will find himself wandering through a maze of disappointments and unmet expectations.

The key questions, stories, and Scriptures in this study will develop your skill, and give you strength and the true basis of a heart for God. Whether you are in the first, second, or third period of the match of life, it is never too late to begin this training of a *Dangerous Man*

As one who has walked through many of the challenges that life can bring, I commend this study to you.

–Jerry E. White, PhD
President Emeritus, The Navigators
March 2006

THANK YOU...

The pages of *The Making of a Dangerous Man LifeJournal* is the reflection of many who have shaped and encouraged me, especially:

Bill Kroeger, for suggesting over lunch the idea of beginning a day's reading in a journal for men with a story of a man.

Jerry White, Dale Eudy, and Chuck Stecker, for your encouragement at the very beginning with the concept of a dangerous man.

Gene Soderberg, for your response, "I think you've got something here."

Cyndee Larson, for your perceptive help in editing the final manuscript.

Jeff Roehrig, Troy Vincent, Bob Morford, Brian Elliott, and Kevin Schulz for helping me develop *The Making of a Dangerous Man* by doing it together, week-by-week.

Neil Anderson, for helping me see the significance of developing a God-rooted identity of who we are in Christ.

Dave Wardell, Kim Gustafson, Chris Van Brocklin, Mike Jordahl, Jim Petersen, and Gaylen Nagel for your encouraging words.

Joe Ehrmann, for your life story written in *A Season of Life* by Jeffrey Marx. The truth "most men compare and compete for their security and significance" was a huge motivational under-pinning of this book.

Ken Ruettgers, for your courage and vulnerability in sharing your challenge in transitioning from professional football with the Green Bay Packers to the next phase of life. When you said, "My greatest issue was the core of my identity," you spoke for the men who have allowed the culture to steal their God-given identity. Thank you for your encouraging words.

Pete Richardson, for taking the time to do the LifePlanning Process with me. Week Ten, your story, reflects your investment in my life.

Jeff Hollenbeck, for your awesome help in developing the cover design.

Christy Daigle, my favorite youngest daughter, for your help in editing—often while feeding our new grandson, Oliver, during the early morning hours.

Maria Hauser, for your servant's heart to help a neophyte author with copyediting and page layout. I am awed by your diligence and persistence!

Art Hauser, for your many thoughtful observations as you helped Maria with her editing. Both of you have incredible servants' hearts!

Shirlee, my wife, for your listening ear and encouragement from the beginning to the end of this project. Your editing was so helpful! You are God's greatest gift to me, other than Christ Himself. *The Making of a Dangerous Man* is the result of your help and encouragement.

There's Danger Ahead!

A man's chief danger is that he is endangered rather than dangerous—and he doesn't realize it. I remember Howard Hendricks, former professor at Dallas Theological Seminary, saying: "Do you know what's scary? It's being influenced by our culture and we are not aware of how we're being influenced!"

As Jerry White warns us in his book *Dangers Men Face*, the dangers we need to fear the most are the ones we do not see until it is too late.[1] Like the frog that is boiled by gradually heating the water, there is danger in the pressures every man faces daily—but they are subtle and unrecognized.

Dangers like:

"The dangers we need to fear the most are the ones we do not see until it is too late."

- busyness and over-activity;
- confusion as to what it means to be a man;
- the tendency to play it safe and the resultant hesitancy to take risks;
- finding our security and significance in the wrong places;
- and our desire for safe distance; prevents us from really connecting with others.

The months and years go by, our sons and daughters grow up before our eyes and then are gone, and we realize our greatest opportunities have passed us by.

The Danger of Identity Theft

Identity theft is increasing at an alarming rate. It is very hard to detect, and by the time you realize your identity has been stolen, the damage has already been done. Loss or theft of a credit card or social security number, results in significant financial loss and stress.

Our enemy, Satan, is not dumb. Through his influence working steadily and undetected through our culture's messages, our identity as God's children eternally loved and accepted by Him is stolen. When our security and significance is no longer God-rooted in the reality of being His children, we have subconsciously bought a lie. We become vulnerable to the lie that our security and significance is determined by our performance, what we own, and what others think about us. We become who the world tells us we are! How driven we can become in our quest for security and significance!

The tragedy then is that we are not free to be dangerous—free to incur any risk to follow Christ and be dangerous (impactful) for God.

How Are You Experiencing the Christian Life?

- "Man, I'm busy—trying to fit in following Christ with my work, family, and church responsibilities."
- "Each week is more of the same. But Christ is in my life and I'm trying to do better."
- "I don't know if I'm passing on to my kids what they need to make it in this world."
- "I hate to admit it, but my life is far more boring and predictable than I would like."
- "I'm not sure I have the inner confidence to follow Christ wherever He would lead me if I gave Him absolute control of my life."
- "I feel more endangered than dangerous!"
- "Following Christ is the greatest, most satisfying risk-demanding adventure I've ever experienced!"

However you identify with the above, God could use this *Dangerous Man LifeJournal* to blow apart your neat, safe view of the Christian life. This could be an explosive experience!

Go ahead and look at the "Contents" page—does it look too simplistic? Don't jump to conclusions too fast!

John Eldredge gifted us with the insight that God created every man with the desire to live for an adventure. What if that heart cry we all have can't be satisfied with our careers, our sports, and our hunting adventures?—I am not saying these things are bad. I greatly enjoy sports: running, weight training, and following the Green Bay Packers.

What if the adventure we long for can only be satisfied in following Christ with a confidence and willingness to risk anything to follow Him? How do you feel about giving absolute control of your life to His leadership? Does this sound threatening?

–To be willing to incur whatever risk He may ask of us takes confidence.

–Confidence breeds risk-taking.

–Where do we get this kind of confidence?

The answers may surprise you and come in ways you never imagined. I have seen this repeated over and over: When a man connects with other men and starts exploring the Bible daily for himself, his heart is transformed. How God will do this specifically in your life, I'm not sure. But He will transform your heart and life in some unexpected ways.

In a scene from the movie *The Rookie*, coach Jim Morris is motivating his baseball team to follow their dreams. He says, "You've got to follow your dreams—you've got to." Then the players turned it back on him: "Coach, what about you?"

Jim Morris had a dream to be a pitcher in the major leagues, but he was injured, and time moved on. So in his mid-thirties he gave up on his dream—until his baseball team challenged him. Jim went to his dad for some advice: should he play it safe and stay a baseball coach, or pursue a tryout with a major league team?

His dad replied, "Your grandfather said: 'It's okay to think about what you want to do until it is time to start doing what you were meant to do.'" And then his dad added, "That may not be what you wanted to hear."

"It's okay to think about what you want to do until it is time to start doing what you were meant to do."

Morris went on to pitch for the Texas Rangers for two years, starting as a 37-year-old rookie.

Maybe you've had the desire in the past to follow Christ with all your heart and pursue the adventure, but you weren't sure what practical steps to take. The gap from where you were and the life you envisioned was too big. So you stayed passive.

Maybe as you are reading this you are thinking, "It's time to start doing what I'm meant to do."

In the following pages you'll find steps to being a dangerous man. Not reckless. Not stupid—but dangerous, in a good way.

Warning: Don't bypass the "Getting Ready" section.

The movie *The Untouchables* tells about Elliott Ness (Kevin Costner) coming to Chicago as a U.S. Treasury agent to get Al Capone. Having grown up in Chicago where my dad once played tennis with the real Elliott Ness, this movie definitely had my attention.

In one scene, Chicago police sergeant Jim Malone (Sean Connery) is in a church talking with Elliott Ness. Malone says, "You said you wanted to know how you could get Capone. Do you really want to get him? Do you see what I'm saying? What are you prepared to do? If you start, you must be prepared to go all the way. You want to get Capone, here's how:

If he pulls a knife, you pull a gun.

If he sends one of your men to the hospital, you send one of his to the morgue.

That's how you get Capone. **Do you want to do that? Are you ready to do that?"**

So maybe you have thought in the past about taking steps to follow Christ with all your heart. Perhaps for one reason or another you have been sidetracked. Now you feel it's time to start doing what you were meant to do.

Do you want to do that? Are you ready to do that?

The "Getting Ready" section will help you answer those questions.

An Example of a Man, Jim Petersen, Who Decided to Go For It...

"I was 21, married, and attending the University of Minnesota. Having discovered the year before that Jesus is, indeed, who He said He is, I was on a mad search to discover how to translate that earthshaking reality into everyday practice. I spent hours in the Scriptures and prayer, searching. Then I came upon Ephesians 3:20:

"Now to him who is able to do far more abundantly than all that we ask or think, according to the power at work within us."

I understood God to be saying: "Jim, Just ask! Just dream! Whatever you come up with—I can do infinitely more than that."

At that, I made a crazy decision. One, which I have lived by ever since. I decided that I would never turn down an opportunity that came my way out of feelings of personal inadequacy. I felt that if I only did those things I knew I could do, anyway, the 'God factor' would be missing in my life. I have been in over my head, operating out of personal weakness ever since. It has been terrifying! But I have experienced the power of God from that day until today. I can't explain what has happened in and through my life in any other terms."

Should I Do *The Making of a Dangerous Man* Alone or With Other Men?

The *Making of a Dangerous Man* is designed for you to do alone or with other men. The "Frequently Asked Questions" section addresses this question. Refer to the "Leader's Guide" if you choose to do it with other men.

Remember: Jesus never promised that following Him would be comfortable or free of risk.

"Stay alert. This is hazardous work I'm assigning you.
You're going to be like sheep running through a wolf pack...
Be as cunning as a snake..." –Matthew 10:16, The Message

GETTING READY

The Making of a Dangerous Man is not about the making of a terrorist, or how the psyche of a criminal is formed.

This is about you and me. You are a dangerous man—either for good or for bad. Every one of us is dangerous in how we impact our families and others. I realize that for our acquaintances (those who are relationally more distant from us)—our influence will be more neutral. But for those in our families and those with whom we work closest, our impact will be either positive or negative.

Yes, you are a dangerous man. So, here's the big question: What makes the difference as to whether our impact on those closest to us will be for better or for worse?

I will never forget the day I read the Bible with astonishment about Paul's experiences:

> *"...Imprisonments, with countless beatings, and often near death... Three times*
> *I was beaten with rods. Once I was stoned. Three times I was shipwrecked;*
> *a night and a day I was adrift at sea; on frequent journeys, in **danger** from*
> *rivers, **danger** from robbers, **danger** from my own people, **danger** from*
> *Gentiles, **danger** in the city, **danger** in the wilderness, **danger** at sea, **danger***
> *from false brothers; in toil and hardship, through many a sleepless night, in*
> *hunger and thirst, often without food, in cold and exposure."*
> –II Corinthians 11:23b-27, ESV

Eight times Paul described himself as in danger. I was perplexed. Why would Paul expose himself over and over to danger, even at the end of his life when men are usually motivated by security and comfort? Why would he keep taking risks? I began looking for clues.

Clue One:

He was committed at the core of his being to following the one, safe leader—Jesus. We can see this by the questions he asked when first confronting Christ:

> *"Who are you, Lord?"* –Acts 22:8
> *"What shall I do, Lord?"* –Acts 22:10

He was committed to following the leadership of Christ.

Clue Two:

Whenever Paul wrote letters, as recorded in the Bible, he inevitably began with either *"Paul, a servant of Christ Jesus,"* or *"Paul, an apostle of Christ Jesus."*

Paul had a rock-solid and God-rooted identity. He knew who he was and whose he was.

He became a dangerous man for good—willing to incur danger and take captives from Satan's rule.

> *"...to open their eyes, so that they may turn from darkness to light and from the power of Satan to God..."* –Acts 26:18, ESV

Before Christ appeared to him, Saul was a dangerous man for bad. He literally ravaged the church, relentlessly entering house after house, dragging men and women off to prison for their professed belief in the Savior (Acts 8:3). He was absolutely convinced that he must oppose the name of Jesus. He not only imprisoned followers of Christ, he voted for their execution. (Acts 26:9-11).

And then he met Christ! He received a new name, Paul, and a new heart. He so grew to treasure Christ as Leader in his heart, that he was willing to risk anything to follow Him. Age had nothing to do with whether he was willing to follow Christ and incur danger.

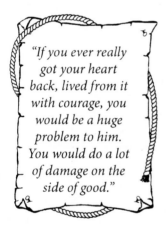

"If you ever really got your heart back, lived from it with courage, you would be a huge problem to him. You would do a lot of damage on the side of good."

John Eldredge in *Wild at Heart* picks up on men being dangerous:

"Do you know why there's been such an assault (on men)? The Enemy fears you. You are dangerous big-time. If you ever really got your heart back, lived from it with courage, you would be a huge problem to him. You would do a lot of damage on the side of good."[1]

"...God made men the way they are because we desperately need them to be the way they are. **Yes, a man is a dangerous thing.** So is a scalpel. It can wound or it can save your life. You don't make it safe by making it dull; you put in the hands of someone who knows what they are doing."[2]

So, what does it mean for you and me to be dangerous for good in the midst of the life circumstances in which we now find ourselves?

The power of someone's story can be incredible. We have included stories of dangerous men who have lived out the reality of following Christ in everyday life. But "your own story" is most important. You have a unique history, and right now God is moving to draw you into the risk and reality of knowing and following Christ.

God is authoring "your story." What often happens is you and I see our lives as a series of events, some good and some bad, some painful and some pleasurable. The tragedy is that we often fail to go beyond the events of our lives to see the meaning, purposes, and glory that God has embedded in those events.

This is a *LifeJournal*: **a place where you can develop and live out "your story" of following Christ in the midst of your life circumstances right now.** I know you may be saying to yourself… "I'm not good at journaling, I've never been a good writer," or "I've never done this before." That's okay. What you need to see is that journaling, the writing out of your thoughts, will help you connect the dots between the events of your life and the incredibly unique story God is authoring in your life now.

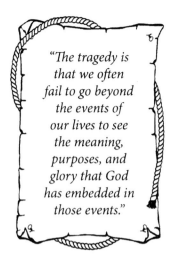

"The tragedy is that we often fail to go beyond the events of our lives to see the meaning, purposes, and glory that God has embedded in those events."

I have to warn you: You must commit yourself to 10-15 minutes every day to read, respond to God in prayer, and record your thoughts in order to see and develop your own story. If you are not ready to commit yourself to do this now, I propose that you don't start. This is not intended to lay a guilt trip on you. If you become sick or unusual events happen resulting in your missing some days, it is not fatal.

However, if you develop the pattern of consistently missing days of connecting with God during time alone, this *LifeJournal* will not work for you. Doing this ten weeks of *The Making of a Dangerous Man* will require an ongoing, heart-level commitment.

John Eldredge states it well. "Most of all, the enemy will try to jam communications with headquarters. Commit yourself to prayer every morning for two weeks and just watch what will happen. You won't want to get up; an important meeting will be called that interferes."[3] –And you could name more hindrances from your experience.

Yes, you are a dangerous man. No doubt about it. You are dangerous for either good or for bad.

The "Ooze Effect"

Ron Martoia says, "Out of the interior life oozes or leaks our attitudes, outlook, irritations, joys, and pain."[4] We have all experienced it—people who have had a toxic, negative impact on you.

The opposite is also true. People who always seem to bring encouragement, high expectation, and a positive spirit. They just ooze and leak that disposition. We can teach what we know, but we will reproduce who we are.

Seeing Ourselves as God Longs for Us to See Ourselves

"Everything we do will flow from how we really perceive ourselves."

This is why we will focus on developing the identity of a dangerous man: everything we do will flow from how we really perceive ourselves. If we do not see ourselves as God longs for us to see ourselves—as His son, then we suffer from a wrong identity of who we really are. And our "leak" on others will be dangerous in a bad way.

Circle Exercise:

We can be dangerous for bad. In the circle below, write the initials of two to three people who impacted you in negative ways in your earlier, formative years.[5]

What did they say or do that so impacted you negatively?

_____

_____

How did they impact you by what they said and did?

_____

_____

Square Exercise:

We can be dangerous for good. Like Paul, like other men. In the square below, write the initials of two to three people who impacted you in a positive way.[6]

What did they say or do that encouraged you and breathed fresh life into your spirit?

_____

_____

How did they impact you by what they said and did?

_____

_____

The Question...

Ten or twenty years from now, will those closest to you (your wife, son, daughter, grandson, son-in-law, nephew, niece, co-workers) be writing your initials in the circle above, or in the square?

As You Begin...

Your story is unique. Where do you think you are now in your journey? Here are some questions for you to assess where you are. Answer each question with a number from 1-10, with 1 being the least true and 10 being the most true:

1. I am prone to play it safe when it comes to following Christ. __
2. I feel very fulfilled in my life. __
3. Life to me is an adventure I relish. __
4. I can see God working in and through my daily relationships. __
5. As a man, I feel secure and significant. __
6. I enjoy reading the Bible, usually daily, and find it very relevant to my life. __
7. I feel confident in conversing about my faith with unbelievers. __
8. I feel busy and like I am operating on fumes. Often I feel hollow, shallow, and enslaved to a schedule that never lets up. __
9. I find myself wanting to control my life and am very hesitant to follow and trust the leadership of Christ in real life. __
10. I feel like I've found a cause that makes me come alive and is bringing out the best in me. __

How would you describe your identity, who you are?

_____

_____

From where do you get your security and significance?

_____

_____

How important to your identity is what you own, what you do (job title), and what others think of you?

_____

_____

I would be jazzed if you would join others and me in helping each other to be dangerous men for good.

The Most Horrible Thing That Could Happen...

Walt Henrichsen, author of *Disciples are Made—Not Born*, asked himself a question one day: What would be the most horrible thing that could happen to him as a Christian? The conclusion he came to was that when he died, God would take him aside and say to him: "Henrichsen, let Me show you what your life could have been like *if only* you had done what I asked, *if* only you had been faithful to me, *if* only you had disciplined your life and made it really count, as I wanted you to."[7]

How can this not happen to us?—By making the radical commitment to becoming a dangerous man.

What Benefits Can You Expect?

- Growth in experiencing security, confidence, and significance as a man that is rooted in the reality of who you are in Christ—not job titles, money, possessions, or sexual prowess;
- Awareness of the false masculinity that permeates the culture in which we live;
- Developing the discipline of a real, daily appointment with God;
- Real friendships and brotherhood as masks and walls come down, if you choose to do *The Making of a Dangerous Man* with other men;
- Increased ability to connect the dots between your life experiences and the unique story that God is authoring in your life;
- The opportunity to grow as a dangerous man for good in the lives of those who mean the most to you;
- Encouragement from stories of dangerous men who incurred risks because they knew who they were as men in Christ, and were willing to follow Him as their Leader.

What is Expected of You?

"For which of you, desiring to build a tower, does not first sit down and count the cost, whether he has enough to complete it? Otherwise, when he has laid a foundation and is not able to finish, all who see it begin to mock him, saying 'This man began to build and was not able to finish.'"
–Luke 14:28–30, ESV

This is the Cost of Commitment to You:

- The heart and willingness to discipline yourself to have a daily appointment with God in His Word;
- The willingness to use *The Making of a Dangerous Man LifeJournal* in your daily appointments with God for six weeks.

If you choose to do *The Making of a Dangerous Man* with other men, the following commitments are critical:

- Make it a priority to be present and on time for weekly meetings. If you cannot make it to a meeting for some reason, contact the group's facilitator before the meeting;
- Actively participate in the discussion, prayer, encouragement, and accountability;
- Be honest with God and with each other.

If this resonates with you, indicate your willingness to commit yourself to the above with your signature and date:

Signed: _____ Date: _____

Note: This is your *LifeJournal*, your story. Make it your own. Personalize and use it in any way that will help you connect the dots between the events of your life and the story God is authoring in your life. Here's a suggestion: keep it with your Bible for the coming weeks and use it to track your thoughts. I'm on your team!

–Al Larson

WEEK THREE

Game Plan

The Challenge

Most men are far more insecure than they like to admit. Mark Goulston, co-author of *The 6 Secrets of a Lasting Relationship*, says: "Inside every man is a secret fear that he lacks competence and courage, that he's not as manly as he should be."[1]

The Goal

See yourself as God longs for you to see yourself—as His son.

The Game Plan

Day 1

"A Man's Career and His Identity" –Ken Ruettgers

Day 2

"A Clear and Present Danger · False Masculinity" –Joe Erhmann

Day 3

"I'm Getting Through it Because I Have a Father in Heaven" –Dave Dravecky

Day 4

"The Impact of Real Masculinity" –Reggie White

Day 5

"Do You Feel God's Pleasure?" –Eric Liddell

Day 6

"Reflection on Week Three"

My Appointment
with God

Best Time

Best Location

WEEK THREE

I am God's Son
Day 1 - "A Man's Career and His Identity"

A Story of a Dangerous Man

Ken Ruettgers was a first round draft pick of the Green Bay Packers in 1985. He was forced to retire in 1996, because of a knee injury. He was on the sidelines during the 1997 Super Bowl when the Packers beat the Patriots 35-21.

If anyone could be a poster boy for how to transition successfully from professional sports to the "real world," it was Ken Ruettgers. He had earned a Master's degree, authored a book, and thought he was ready to transition successfully.

Experience proved otherwise. After leaving football, he could barely get out of bed and take a shower. His thought was, "Hey, what do I have to live for? My best days are gone."

"My greatest issue was the core of my identity," said Ruettgers. "A fan will come up in Green Bay when I'm there and say, 'Don't tell me. Didn't you used to be Ken Ruettgers?' Well, yeah, I think I still am, but I'm not really sure."[1]

What happened to Ken happens to many of us. Our identity is so defined by what we do for a job or a career, that when our job changes or is eliminated our identity becomes devastated.

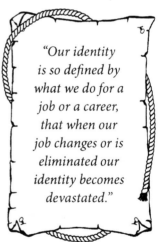

"Our identity is so defined by what we do for a job or a career, that when our job changes or is eliminated our identity becomes devastated."

Loss of motivation, depression, emotional paralysis, spending sprees, substance abuse, and even suicide are common effects.

Ken is now the executive director of GamesOver.org, a resource to help professional athletes successfully retire and transition to the next phase of their lives.

Read John 1:9–13

Respond:

1. What happens when we live in darkness?

2. How does one not become a child of God?

3. How does a person enter God's family and become His son?

4. What does it mean to "receive Christ"?

Your Story:

Was there a time in your life when you experienced something like Ken Ruettgers—a job change or other transition that wreaked havoc with your identity and seriously impacted you?

Describe how you feel, where you are in your journey. Do you believe in your heart you are a son of God, or do you feel you are in the process of coming to grips with this?

If you believe you are God's son, describe the time in your life when you received Christ and became His son.

Week Three

I am God's Son
Day 2 - "A Clear and Present Danger - False Masculinity"

A Story of a Dangerous Man

Joe Ehrmann coaches a winning high school football team, not based on a tough-guy ideal but on a different way of defining what manhood means. He played professional football for 13 years, most of them as a defensive lineman for the Baltimore Colts.

"The single greatest crisis is to answer the question, 'What does it mean to be a man?' The culture is giving our boys a threefold criterion for what it means: athletic ability, sexual conquest, and economic success. It causes men to compare what we have and compete with others for what they have."[1]

He further illustrates this by noting how boys compare their athletic abilities to others and compete for whatever attention it brings. As they move into their teen years, they compare their girlfriends with their friends' girlfriends and compete for the status of having the coolest girl. As adults, we compare bank accounts and job titles, houses and cars, and compete for the security and power that those represent.

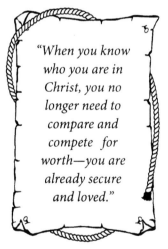

"*When you know who you are in Christ, you no longer need to compare and compete for worth—you are already secure and loved.*"

"We compare, we compete. That's all we ever do—from the ball fields—to the bedroom—to the billfold. It leaves men isolated, alone, feeling insecure, and insignificant. It sabotages relationships of community from the get-go."[2]

But when you know who you are in Christ, you no longer need to compare and compete for worth—you are already secure and loved.[3] You are free to be dangerous!

Read Galatians 4:4-7

Respond:

1. Why did God send His Son to redeem you?

_____

_____

2. Therefore, what relationship do you think God intends to be at the core of your identity?

_____

_____

3. What has God done to affirm your sonship?

_____

_____

Your Story:

What is your definition of masculinity as you begin _The Making of a Dangerous Man_?

_____

_____

What did your father communicate to you as to what it means to be a man?

_____

_____

How did your father's definition of masculinity impact you?

_____

_____

WEEK THREE

I am God's Son
Day 3 - "I'm Getting Through It Because I Have a Father in Heaven"

A Story of a Dangerous Man

Dave Dravecky pitched for the San Diego Padres, made the All-Star team, and played in the play-offs and World Series. In the fall of 1987, he noticed a small lump on his arm. He pitched well until the beginning of the next season. By then the lump on his arm was as big as a golf ball.

Tests showed the lump to be a cancerous tumor that needed to be removed. During a thirteen-hour operation, a surgeon removed half of his deltoid muscle and froze his bone to kill the cancer cells.

No one expected Dave to ever pitch again, but he did. During the second game of his comeback, his arm broke. The cancer was back, requiring a second operation, more radiation, infection, and pain. After all this, the tumor was back again, resulting in the amputation of his arm and shoulder. Simple tasks like tying his shoes and buttoning his clothes became difficult for the all-star pitcher.

When asked how he kept from getting bitter, he said, "I'm not getting through the loss of my arm because I am a great coper. I'm getting through it because I have a Father in heaven Who is a great giver. At the time I need strength, He puts it in my heart."[1]

Read Ephesians 1:3-6

Respond:

1. How is God described in verse 3?

_____

_____

2. When did God choose you?

_____

_____

3. What does God's choosing you imply about Him?

4. What motivated God to adopt you?

Your Story:

What is one of the most painful experiences you have gone through—physically and/or emotionally?

What enabled you to get through that experience?

Were you tempted to become bitter?

What did you learn about God from the experience?

How do you think God intends to bring about good through that experience?

WEEK THREE

I am God's Son
Day 4 · "The Impact of Real Masculinity"

A Story of a Dangerous Man

Reggie White was an incredible football player with the Philadelphia Eagles, and later the Green Bay Packers. The signing of Reggie White as a free agent (combined with the trade for Brett Favre) comprised a turning point in the history of the Green Bay Packers franchise.

Reggie died unexpectedly on December 28, 2003, from a lung disease. The impact of his loss was felt deeply—especially by his teammates. Next to his immediate family, Reggie's loss may have been felt the most by Gilbert Brown, who anchored the middle of the line as nose tackle while Reggie played with the Packers.

"He always told me how much he loved me and cared about me. That's why his death hurts so much," Brown says. "Everything he did, I watched and I tried to do. I looked up at him like I was his son and he was my father. He led by example. He led mentally. He led physically. I've seen that man throw grown men around the field like they were rag dolls, and he'd be the first one to help them up."

"Off the field, the kindest thing Reggie ever did for me was to tell me how to be a man. Reggie was everything to me."[1]

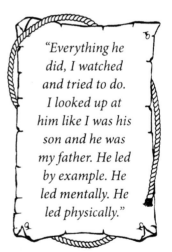

"Everything he did, I watched and tried to do. I looked up at him like I was his son and he was my father. He led by example. He led mentally. He led physically."

Read Romans 8:14-16

Respond:

1. According to verse 14, who are sons of God?

_____

_____

2. What does it mean to you to be "led by the Spirit of God"?

3. According to verse 15, what kind of spirit have we received?

4. How does one gain confidence of his sonship with his Heavenly Father? ✱

Your Story:

Who has been a great example of what it means to be a man to you?

Do you have confidence and assurance that you are God's son?

Do you feel that assurance in the inner recesses of your spirit?

Which would you say characterizes your life more: allowing God's Spirit to direct your life or holding back from fear?

✱ *"God's Spirit touches our spirit and confirms who we really are. We know who we are: Father and children."* –Romans 8:16, The Message

WEEK THREE

I am God's Son
Day 5 - "Do You Feel God's Pleasure?"

A Story of a Dangerous Man

Eric Liddell became known more for what he didn't do than for what he did. Eric was a very fast runner. After becoming the British champion in the 100-meter sprint, he planned to enter this event in the 1924 Olympics. But shortly before the Olympics began, when he heard the race would be held on a Sunday, he said he wouldn't compete. He believed Sunday should be a day to rest and focus on the Lord.

Although there wasn't much time left before the Olympics, he began training for the quarter-mile race, which wouldn't be held on a Sunday. God enabled him not only to win the quarter-mile race, but also to set a world record.[1]

In the movie *Chariots of Fire*, Eric's Olympic aspirations are opposed by his sister, Jenny. She fears that his success as a runner will turn him away from going to China as a missionary. Liddell tells her, "I'm going to China, Jenny, but you've got to understand. I believe God made me for a purpose, for China. But He also made me fast. When I run, I feel His pleasure."[2]

Read Matthew 3:13-4:4

Respond:

1. Why do you think the Father said, "This is my beloved Son, with whom I am well pleased" (verse 3:17) immediately before He was led into the wilderness to be tempted by the devil?

_____

_____

2. Note how the devil repeatedly began his tempting with the enticement of Jesus to question his identity (verses 4:3 and 4:6).

_____

_____

3. What do you think is the connection between the Father's affirmation in Matthew 3:17 and the devil's subsequent temptations beginning with the questioning of Jesus' identity?

Your Story:

Have you experienced your Heavenly Father impressing on you the thought "(insert your name), I am so pleased with you, you are My son whom I love"?

Why do you think it would be significant for us to hear God express His affirmation? Do you think our hearing God say this to us impacts our sense of security and significance?

Eric Liddell said, "When I run, I feel God's pleasure." In the midst of what you do during the course of the day, do you feel the pleasure God has in you?

Have you ever heard your own dad express how he felt about you? —Statements like: "I am so proud of you, I am so glad you are my son, I do love you." How did his expressing or not expressing how he felt about you impact you?

Do those closest to you (wife, son, etc.) hear from you how you feel about them?

WEEK THREE

I am God's son
Day 6 - "Reflection on the Week"

Our New Identity

"Put on the new self, which is being renewed in knowledge after the image of its Creator. Here there is not Greek and Jew, circumcised and uncircumcised, barbarian, Scythian, slave, free; but Christ is all, and in all."
–Colossians, 3:10–11, ESV

When people are asked to describe themselves, usually they mention race, religion, cultural background, job, or other social distinctions. Paul says that when it comes to our core identity, these descriptions no longer apply. Our fundamental identity is that we are children of God. We are in Christ.

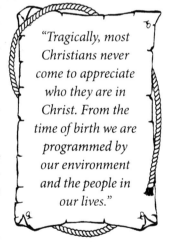

"Tragically, most Christians never come to appreciate who they are in Christ. From the time of birth we are programmed by our environment and the people in our lives."

Neil Anderson, in the Living Free in Christ conference, says: "Tragically, most Christians *never* come to appreciate who they are in Christ. From the time of birth we are programmed by our environment and the people in our lives. For the many who have experienced rejection, abandonment, and abuse from early childhood, entrenched are attitudes such as, 'I am of no value, I don't measure up, and I am unlovable.'"[1]

It is so easy to forget our identity in Christ! Satan does not want you to live in the freedom of your identity in Christ. So how do you remember to live in the midst of real life, consciously aware of your identity as a son of God?

"Do not be conformed to this world, but be transformed by the renewal of your mind ..."
–Romans 12:2, ESV

The inner transformation of our minds doesn't come naturally or quickly. There is no "delete" button that instantly erases past programming. But real transformation can happen. It can happen through daily appointments with God in His Word. When it does, He can cleanse our thinking and spirit by His truth.

A Few Dangerous Questions...

Did it work for you this past week to make space in your life to connect with your Heavenly Father in a real way for 10-15 minutes a day, or most days?

If not, what changes do you need to make?

Was there a time during the past week when God impressed upon you to say or do something, but responding would have taken you out of your comfort zone?

How did you respond?

Reflect Over Your Journaling the Past Week...

What was the week's "take-away"—the most important truth God impressed on you or an action step for you to take?

Pray Over the Week's "Take-away"...

Ask the Holy Spirit to embed the most significant thought or truth in your mind and spirit this coming week in a way that will help you consciously live in the shadow of that truth. Pray over any action step God has impressed on you.

WEEK FOUR

Game Plan

The Challenge

Unmask the influence of the world and our enemy for what it is: manipulative, controlling, and destructive in the way we value and view ourselves.

The Goal

See yourself as God longs for you to see yourself: as His son, forever and unconditionally loved by your Heavenly Father. Keep saying this coming week "Thank you, God, for choosing me to be your son and loving me unconditionally."

The Game Plan

Day 1

"How Do I Win God's Favor?" –Martin Luther

Day 2

"Disfigured but Marked by God's Love" –Dave Roever

Day 3

"A Man of Raging Fury is Changed Forever" –Apostle Paul

Day 4

"What Can Separate Us From God's Love?" –Dennis Byrd

Day 5

"Beaten But Not Bitter" –John Perkins

Day 6

"Reflection on Week Four"

My Appointment
with God

Best Time

Best Location

I am Loved by God - Forever and Unconditionally
Day 1 - "How Do I Win God's Favor?"

A Story of a Dangerous Man

God used **Martin Luther** to change the history of Christianity and the world. Luther attended a university in Germany to become a lawyer. But from childhood, he had been afraid of dying and facing God's judgment. He desperately wanted to know what he had to do to win God's love and favor.

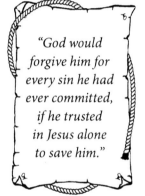

After being knocked down by a bolt of lightning, Martin was terrified and promised to be a monk so he could earn his way to heaven. Even after fasting and doing other things to earn God's favor, he was overwhelmed with feelings of guilt. He never felt good enough to earn God's love.

"God would forgive him for every sin he had ever committed, if he trusted in Jesus alone to save him."

He became a teacher and was assigned to teach the Bible at the University of Wittenberg. While teaching from the book of Romans, he found the answer to his quest: God would forgive him for every sin he had ever committed, if he trusted in Jesus alone to save him.

At the time, there were few Bibles, and those were printed in Latin, which the common people could not read. There was only one church—Roman Catholic, which taught that people must follow certain rules to obtain God's blessing. Martin wanted everyone to know what he discovered, so he nailed 95 statements of what the Bible said about the forgiveness of sins on the door of a large church. This caused his life to be threatened and forced him to hide. It was while he was hiding that he translated the New Testament into German so everyone could read it.[1]

Read Romans 5:8 and 8:31-34

Respond:

1. What does the fact that Christ died for us when we were sinners tell us about the character of God's love for us?

_____

_____

2. What are the implications of the truth that "God is for us" (8:32-33)?

_____

_____

3. According to Romans 8:33-34, what must be our response to Satan's condemning accusations?

_____

_____

Your Story:

Was there a time in your life when you experienced something like Martin Luther—the fear of death and the frustration of wanting to do enough to win God's love?

_____

_____

Have you come to the place where you do not feel pressured to perform well in order to be accepted by God?

_____

_____

I am Loved by God - Forever and Unconditionally
Day 2 - "Disfigured But Marked by God's Love"

A Story of a Dangerous Man

Dave Roever did so well in the Navy's basic training that he was chosen to train for river patrol—a very dangerous assignment in Vietnam at the time. It was his patrol's job to move up and down a river to look for Communist soldiers.

While on patrol one day, Dave prepared to throw a special grenade designed to burn jungle brush and expose booby traps. The grenade was defective and blew up in his hand. Dave's body caught fire and continued to burn even though he dove into the river. Third-degree burns covered 40 percent of his body. He almost died.

When he saw himself in a mirror during his recovery, Dave felt like a monster— half his face was gone. He had experienced excruciating physical pain, along with the emotional pain caused by others' reactions of shock and fear. His wife stood with him and loved him regardless of his appearance.

Dave has struggled with feeling unacceptable. But he has also experienced a deep sense of worth in God's never-ending love. This love gives him the confidence and drive to travel the world holding crusades and telling others of God's love and sufficiency.[1]

Read I John 4:10-18

Respond:

1. Was God's love caused by us?

_____

_____

If not, what caused God to love us?

_____

_____

2. How do we come to know and experience God's love for us? (verse 16)

_____

_____

3. When we are controlled by fear, what does that reveal?

_____

_____

Your Story:

What have you experienced that caused you to seriously question God's love for you?

_____

_____

Have you come to the place where you trust the love God has for you?

_____

_____

WEEK FOUR

I am Loved by God - Forever and Unconditionally
Day 3 - "A Man of Raging Fury is Changed Forever"

A Story of a Dangerous Man

The **apostle Paul** was a very dangerous guy! When Stephen was being stoned, there was Saul (his earlier name, Acts 7:58). Saul literally ravaged the early church, relentlessly entering house after house, and dragging men and women off to prison for their faith in Christ (Acts 8:3). He was absolutely convinced that he must oppose the name of Jesus. He not only imprisoned followers of Christ, he voted for their execution. In a raging fury, he tried to make them speak evil of Christ and sought to persecute them wherever they sought escape (Acts 26:9-11).

The turning point in Saul's life was when he met Christ on the Damascus Road and asked two questions:

"Who are you, Lord?" and

"What shall I do, Lord?" –Acts 22:8-10

He received a new name, Paul, and a new heart.

Read below to discover what became the compelling factor in Paul's life. As a result, the history of Christianity was unalterably changed. Paul brought the Gospel to the Gentiles and to the non-Jewish world—which eventually enabled you and I to access God Himself!

Read II Corinthians 5:14-15 and Philippians 3:4-10

Respond:

1. According to II Corinthians 5:14-15, was it God's love for Paul or Paul's love for Christ that controlled and impelled him?✹

_____

_____

Briefly explain your response.

_____

_____

2. What is one reason Christ died for you?

_____

_____

3. According to Philippians 3:7-9, how were Paul's values forever impacted?

_____

_____

Your Story:

It is common knowledge that _"God so loved the world that He gave His only son..."_
–John 3:16. But do you feel that the truth of God's love for you has ever permeated
your heart and spirit in a real way?

_____

_____

If so, describe how God's favor and love became real to you.

_____

_____

❋ _"For the love of Christ controls and urges and impels us..."_
–II Corinthians 5:14, Amplified Bible

I am Loved by God - Forever and Unconditionally
Day 4 - "What Can Separate Us From God's Love?"

A Story of a Dangerous Man

It all happened at Giants Stadium on November 29, 1992, when **Dennis Byrd** charged the Kansas City Chiefs' quarterback. Just before he was about to make the tackle, the quarterback stepped forward. Dennis's 6 feet 5 inches tall, 270-pound body collided with his 280-pound teammate, and his neck shattered. It happened so fast that he wasn't able to position his head correctly to absorb the hit.

It has been said that in many of our lives there is a defining "before" and "after." Before the accident, Dennis could bench-press 430 pounds and squat-lift 800. He was one of the Jets' most popular players, carefree and full of pranks.

After the accident, he had to ask nurses and attendants to do everything for him. He had to be turned every two hours to keep ulcers from forming on his skin. It would take him many hours to relearn how to do simple tasks such as brushing his teeth and combing his hair.

During an interview with Bob Costas before the Super Bowl game between the Cowboys and Bills, he expressed what enabled him to keep going: "Without question the biggest factor in my life has been my faith in Jesus Christ. That's been able to keep me going. God's given me the strength every day."[1]

"Without question, the biggest factor in my life has been my faith in Jesus Christ. That's been able to keep me going. God's given me the strength every day."

Read Romans 8:31-39

Respond:

1. In verses 35-39 Paul identifies what can never separate us from the love of God in Christ. What are the things that cannot sever us from the love God has for us?

_____

_____

2. Paul says, "...in all these things we are more than conquerors." How can this be?

_____

_____

Your Story:

Have you ever had a defining experience that became for you a "before" and an "after"?

_____

_____

If so, what was that experience?

_____

_____

Regarding the above experience, what kept you going?

_____

_____

Did you become bitter?

_____

_____

Did you experience God in new ways?

_____

_____

> *"The One who died for us—who was raised to life for us, is in the presence of God at this very moment sticking up for us. Do you think anyone is going to be able to drive a wedge between us and Christ's love for us? There is no way! Not trouble, not hard times..."*
> –Romans 8:34-37, The Message

WEEK FOUR

I am Loved by God - Forever and Unconditionally
Day 5 - "Beaten But Not Bitter"

A Story of a Dangerous Man

When **John Perkins** walked to school as a child in Mississippi, he would hear white children holler, "Move off the road, nigger!" And then they would throw rocks at him. Whites had a school bus and didn't have to walk for miles to school like black children.[1]

"Tail kicking" was common practice in Mississippi. White men would look for a black man to pick on, and when they found someone, they would kick him on his backside. It was humiliating—the victim would run away with the sound of people laughing in his ears. When a large white man kicked John's brother, Clyde, he picked himself up and decked his tormentor with one punch. Later Clyde was shot and killed in retaliation by a local marshal. John burned with anger.[2]

In 1947, John moved to California because of beckoning opportunity. He worked alongside whites and received the same wages! (Cheating blacks was common practice in Mississippi). John married his wife, Vera Mae, in 1951. In the spring of 1957, their son Spencer began attending a children's Bible class at a little church close to home.

One day, Spencer asked "Daddy, will you come to church with me?" John couldn't refuse his son. In church, the preacher taught a lesson about God's love. For the first time in his life, he heard a new idea about God—that God loved John Perkins. Then he started attending a Tuesday night Bible study. Soon after, John made a decision to follow Christ with his life.[3]

"Though beaten, John never gave in to hate. Instead he focused on the love of God and asked God to fill his heart with that same love."

John had a nice home and economic success in California. But he heard God's voice: "Come back to Mississippi and help your people."[4] In 1961, he and his family moved back to Mississippi and began the Berean Bible Church and Voice of Calvary Ministries.

Nine years later John was beaten and almost died in the Brandon, Mississippi jail. The local police hated John and his friends who were organizing efforts for fair treatment of blacks. Though beaten, John never gave in to hate. Instead he focused on the love of God and asked God to fill his heart with that same love.[5]

Read Lamentations 3:21-25

Respond:

1. When does the flow of God's love and mercy stop for you?

2. How often does God express His love and mercies to you?

3. What is the source of our hope?

Your Story:

How has God shown his love and mercies to you recently?

Spend some time in prayer thanking God for the way He has expressed his love and mercies to you.

WEEK FOUR

I am Loved by God - Forever and Unconditionally
Day 6 - "Reflection on the Week"

Crossing the Abyss – From Head to Heart

In his book *Rabbi's Heartbeat*, Brennan Manning confesses, "The great divorce between my head and my heart endured throughout my ministry. For 18 years I proclaimed the good news of God's passionate, unconditional love—utterly convicted in my head but not feeling it in my heart. I never felt loved. But finally..."[1]

Manning tells the story of a high school teacher by the name of John Egan who spent 30 years ministering to youth. He kept a journal that was published shortly after his death in 1987. During his annual, eight-day directed retreat he was visiting with the one directing his time:

"The heart of it is this: To make the Lord and His immense love for you constitutive of your personal worth. Define yourself radically as one beloved by God."

"[*The director*] states something that I will ponder for years; he says it very deliberately. I ask him to repeat it so that I can write it down. 'John, the heart of it is this: to make the Lord and His immense love for you constitutive of your personal worth. Define yourself radically as one beloved by God. God's love for you and His choice of you constitute your worth. Accept that, and let it become the most important thing in your life.'

"We discuss it. The basis of my personal worth is not my possessions, my talents, not esteem of others, reputation—not kudos of appreciation from parents and kids, not applause, and everyone telling you how important you are to the place—I stand anchored now in God before whom I stand naked, this God who tells me, '**You are my son, my beloved one.**'"[2]

As I have interacted over this with other friends and Christian leaders, one said, "That's not where I live!"—Precisely! This is our challenge: to cross the abyss of truth we know in a cerebral way so that we can come to trust and live in the truth of God's love for you and me. How can this happen? I'm not aware of any magic formula, but the distance could be shortened with a simple prayer:

"Holy Spirit, help me to grasp the truth that You love me as Your son— forever and unconditionally. Help me so to grasp this truth in the depths of my spirit so that even in the midst of daily life experiences I will not forget your total acceptance and love for me. Help me hear with my heart what you have to say to me about being Your son who gives You great pleasure."

Do you have a son or daughter, or granddaughter or grandson, that you just enjoy being with? Does looking at their picture bring an inner smile and pleasure? You keep pictures of them in your kitchen, office, and wallet. In the same way, you bring a unique pleasure to your Heavenly Father!

God longs for you to see yourself as His son, forever and unconditionally loved by your Heavenly Father. It must grieve Him when we succumb to the pressure of the world and compare and compete with others for our worth and security. **Let His love for you define who you are.**

A Prayer from Paul That You Could Pray...

"My response is to get down on my knees before the Father, this magnificent Father who parcels out all heaven and earth. I ask him to strengthen you by his Spirit—not a brute strength but a glorious inner strength—that Christ will live in you as you open the door and invite him in. And I ask him that... you'll be able to take in... the extravagant dimensions of Christ's love. Reach out and experience the breadth! Test its length! Plumb the depths! Rise to the heights! Live full lives, full in the fullness of God." –Ephesians 3:14-19, The Message

A Few Dangerous Questions...

Did it work for you this past week to make space in your life to connect with your Heavenly Father in a real way for 10-15 minutes a day, or most days?

If not, what changes do you need to make?

Was there a time during the past week when God impressed upon you to say or do something, but responding would have taken you out of your comfort zone?

How did you respond?

_____

_____

Reflect on Your Journaling the Past Week...

What was the week's "take-away"—the most important truth God impressed on you or an action step for you to take?

_____

_____

Pray Over the Week's "Take-away"...

Ask the Holy Spirit to embed the most significant thought or truth in your mind and spirit this coming week in a way that will help you consciously live in the shadow of that truth. Pray over any action step God has impressed on you.

WEEK FIVE

Game Plan

The Challenge

To recognize and actively confront the condemning, accusing attacks of our enemy. These attacks rob us of enjoying our acceptance by God and thwart us from freely and boldly following the leadership of Christ.

The Goal

To appreciate and enjoy our acceptance and security as the son of our sovereign, Heavenly Father in the midst of life's circumstances.

The Game Plan

Day 1

"God-rooted Acceptance Gives Freedom" –A.C. Green

Day 2

"I Am Forever Free From Condemnation" –Neil Anderson

Day 3

"From Insecurity to God's Word to Hope" –John Piper

Day 4

"A Dangerous Man Knows to Whom He Belongs" –Dietrich Bonhoeffer

Day 5

"The Joy of a Dangerous Man" –Tim Hansel

Day 6

"Reflection on Week Five"

My Appointment
with God

Best Time

Best Location

WEEK FIVE

I am Accepted and Secure
Day 1 - "God-rooted Acceptance Gives Freedom"

A Story of a Dangerous Man

Until high school, **A. C. Green** was average in size. Then he had a real growth spurt. By the time he graduated from high school, he was 6 feet 7 inches tall. One day his high school basketball coach, coach Gray, put his hand on Green's shoulder and encouraged him to stick with it because of his potential to succeed in the future.

A.C. averaged 27 points a game as a senior and was named Player of the Year in Oregon. But in spite of his athletic success, A.C. felt insecure. He was fearful of making decisions and relied on other people to tell him how good he was.

Through the influence of a former teacher, he went to a church where he heard clearly how he could personally relate to God. After he committed his life to Christ, he felt free for the first time. He no longer was dependent on other people's opinions for emotional security.

After starring for Oregon State University, he was drafted by the Los Angeles Lakers. There he had the opportunity to play with Magic Johnson and Kareem Abdul-Jabbar. A.C. had made a promise to God that he wouldn't have sex before marriage. Can you imagine the ribbing he took from other players about his conviction! He and other friends developed the organization Athletes for Abstinence to challenge kids that sex outside of marriage is destructive and dangerous.[1]

Read Romans 15:7 and I Corinthians 4:1-4

Respond:

1. According to Romans 15:7, Christ has accepted and welcomed us.
   How does Christ's acceptance of us relate to our striving for the acceptance and approval of others?

_____

_____

2. In I Corinthians 4:1-4, Paul shared that the judgment of others wasn't a big concern of his. What gave Paul the freedom to not be controlled by what others thought?

_____

_____

Your Story:

Do you feel accepted by God?

_____

_____

Do you feel a need to strive for the acceptance and approval of others?

_____

_____

WEEK FIVE

I am Accepted and Secure
Day 2 · "I am Forever Free from Condemnation"

A Story of a Dangerous Man

Dr. Neil Anderson was an aerospace engineer before entering the professional Christian ministry. He was born and raised on a farm in Minnesota, where his social life centered on family, school, and church. He was 25 years old before he realized who God is and why Jesus came.

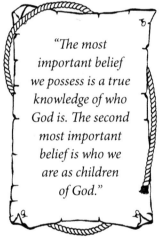

"*The most important belief we possess is a true knowledge of who God is. The second most important belief is who we are as children of God.*"

It would be another 15 years before he finally realized who he was as a child of God. Neil believes that the most important belief we possess is a true knowledge of who God is. The second most important belief is who we are as children of God.

It was while teaching at the Talbot School of Theology at Biola University, that he and his wife, Joanne, experienced a life-changing crisis. For 15 months he wasn't sure if Joanne was going to live or die. They were not able to get an accurate medical diagnosis of her condition. As a result they lost everything because they had to pay for medical expenses. The turning point was when Biola University had a day of prayer. During that time God brought Neil to the end of his human resources so he could discover God's resources. Freedom in Christ Ministries was born out of this brokenness.[1]

Neil's books include *The Daily Discipler, Victory Over the Darkness*, and *The Bondage Breaker*. In the early 1990's, I attended a *Freedom in Christ* conference in Minneapolis where Neil spoke. *The Making of a Dangerous Man* is largely the result of what God impressed on me at that time: the significance of developing a God-rooted identity as God's child/son. Through his books and speaking in conferences like this, God has given thousands of people a new freedom through finding their true identity and sense of worth in Christ.[2]

Read Romans 8:1-2,33-34, and Revelation 12:10

Respond:

1. On what basis are we free from condemnation and the power (law) of sin?

2. How should we respond to the condemning accusations from our enemy, Satan?

Your Story:

Do you find yourself believing and succumbing to condemning thoughts?

Thank God for freeing you from eternal condemnation through what Christ has done for you.

WEEK FIVE

I am Accepted and Secure
Day 3 - "From Insecurity to God's Word to Hope"

A Story of a Dangerous Man

John Piper was a 34-year-old professor at Bethel University when he was called by Bethlehem Baptist Church in Minneapolis, Minnesota to be senior pastor. He had never performed a wedding or a funeral, and at times felt unprepared and insecure as senior pastor. In his seminary training, he had focused on the Bible and had not taken practical courses related to the routine functioning of a church.

One day John was called to the hospital where the grieving husband of his seriously ill wife asked him to give them a word from the Lord. His mind went blank, but he was able to "mumble something" in prayer, as John describes the experience.

John was devastated by his own response, and determined that it would never happen again. He memorized Psalm 46, and kept putting his hope in God. He had a huge sign placed on the church building: **HOPE IN GOD.**[1]

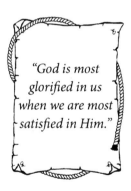

"God is most glorified in us when we are most satisfied in Him."

John's insecurities drove him to the Scriptures and to focus his hope on God alone. His life message, "God is most glorified in us when we are most satisfied in Him," has encouraged Christ-followers around the world to embrace Christ as their greatest joy and treasure.

Read Psalm 46:1-10
Respond:

1. How is God described?

_____

_____

2. What are the implications for my life?

_____

_____

Your Story:

Are there circumstances in your life now that cause you to feel insecure?

_____

_____

What truth about God can you anchor your hope upon?

_____

_____

Is there any specific step God wants you to take to cooperate with Him?

_____

_____

WEEK FIVE

I am Accepted and Secure
Day 4 - "A Dangerous Man Knows to Whom He Belongs"

A Story of a Dangerous Man

Dietrich Bonhoeffer was hanged by special order at the German concentration camp at Flossenburg on April 9, 1945, just a few days before the Allies liberated it. In 1933, he had denounced Hitler and his ideas. Two years later, he was forbidden to teach and was banned from Berlin by Nazi authorities. In 1935, he returned to Germany from England to direct an illegal Church Training College to train pastors.[1]

At the outbreak of World War II, he was in the U.S. on a lecture tour. While in New York, he kept asking God "What shall I do?" And the answer kept coming back "Go back to Germany."[2] Against the advice of his friends, he gave up the security of the U.S. and returned to Germany to work for the church and the political opposition to Hitler. The Gestapo arrested him in his parents' home on April 5, 1943.[3] He spent the next two years in prison and concentration camps until his execution in 1945.

Bill Hull said, "If you're a fearful person, you can't follow Jesus in the way He wants you to go."[4] So, what gave Bonhoeffer the courage and security to follow Christ in the path of danger? He leaves us a clue in one of the letters and papers smuggled out of prison. In his paper "Who Am I?," he struggles with who he is and concludes with: "Who am I? Whoever I am, Thou knowest, O God, **I am thine!**"[5]

Knowing to whom he ultimately belonged to gave him the security to follow Christ, regardless of the danger that awaited him.

"Knowing who he ultimately belonged to gave him the security to follow Christ, regardless of the danger that awaited him."

Read I Corinthians 6:19-20 and 7:23

Respond:

1. How are we to regard our bodies and our lives?

2. Why are we to regard ourselves in this way?

Your Story:

Do you view yourself (including your body) as sacred "territory"?

Do you sometimes feel captive more to people's opinions than to God Himself?

Week Five

I am Accepted and Secure
Day 5 · "The Joy of a Dangerous Man"

A Story of a Dangerous Man

In 1970, **Tim Hansel** started Summit Expedition, an organization that takes kids and adults on mountain climbing and wilderness survival trips. The purpose of these trips is for the participants to accomplish more than they thought they could, and in the process to know themselves and God better.

The turning point in Tim's life came on a mountain-climbing trip in the Sierras. After he and a couple of friends scaled a 14,000-foot mountain, they started the descent. On the way down, Tim's boots became packed with snow and ineffective for gripping. He slipped and fell, and landed upside down on his neck fifty–some feet below. He had to climb out of the crevasse and hike over 20 miles to his car. He then drove himself home!

At the hospital, X-rays showed fractured bones and crushed discs in his spine, and broken pieces of bone in his neck. Since that time, he cannot remember a single morning where he could wake up and feel well. Tim was told he would have to learn to live with never-ending pain.

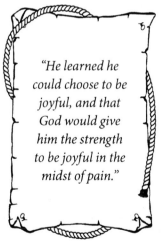

"He learned he could choose to be joyful, and that God would give him the strength to be joyful in the midst of pain."

Over time, Tim has learned to respond to the continuous pain. Through Bible verses like Nehemiah 8:10, he learned he could choose to be joyful, and that God would give him the strength to be joyful in the midst of pain. He found joy to be rooted in his sovereign God that is in control of every area of his life.[1]

Read Nehemiah 8:9-12, Genesis 45:8, 50:20, and Romans 8:28

Respond:

1. According to Nehemiah, where does our strength come from?

_____

_____

2. How did Joseph see God's hand in the cruel ways his brothers treated him?

_____

_____

Your Story:

Do you think that God is in control of the events of your life?

_____

_____

Do you really believe God is causing all things in your life to work together for your good?

_____

_____

Do you enjoy God?

_____

_____

WEEK FIVE

I am Accepted and Secure
Day 6 · "Reflection on the Week"

J.I. Packer, in his book, *Knowing God*, asks the question, "What is a Christian? The richest answer I know is that a Christian is one who has God for his Father." As we have seen from several places in the Bible, our sonship is a gift of grace—not a natural, but an "adoptive" sonship.[1]

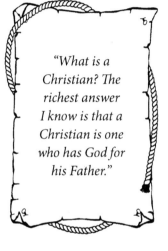

"What is a Christian? The richest answer I know is that a Christian is one who has God for his Father."

My daughter Rachel and her husband Kevin, adopted a little girl from China. Their baby, Holly, was found at the entrance to an electrical plant in China. She was born September 8, 2001, three days before the fateful flight of planes into the Twin Towers of New York.

They adopted her because they wanted her. And they totally delight in her. To see Holly's and Rachel's faces brighten upon meeting after being separated from a day of work shouts mutual delight. The separation is over!

Rachel and Kevin's adopting Holly out of desire and delight helps me feel what God's adoption of you and I is like. Packer describes it like this: "Adoption, by its very nature, is an act of free kindness to the person adopted. If you become a father by adopting a child, you do so because you choose to, not because you are bound to. Similarly, God adopts us because He chooses to. He had no duty to do so. He did not need to do anything about our sins except punish us as we deserved. But He loved us; so He redeemed us, forgave us, took us as His sons, and gave Himself to us as our Father."[2]

Jesus describes the security of His followers:

> *"My sheep hear my voice, and I know them, and they follow me. I give them eternal life, and they will never perish, and no one will snatch them out of hand. My Father, who has given them to me, is greater than all, and no one is able to snatch them out of the Father's hand."* –John 10:27-29, ESV

Here's the point of our previous weeks of reading: Do I know my own real identity?

I am a child of God. God is my Father. Keep saying it to yourself first thing in the morning, and last thing at night.[3] This is the most secure place you can be: a son in your Father's hand.

A Few Dangerous Questions...

Did it work for you this past week to make space in your life to connect with your Heavenly Father in a real way for 10-15 minutes a day, or most days?

_____

_____

If not, what changes do you need to make?

_____

_____

Was there a time during the past week when God impressed upon you to say or do something, but responding would have taken you out of your comfort zone?

_____

_____

How did you respond?

_____

_____

Reflect Over Your Journaling the Past Week...

What was the week's "take-away"—the most important truth God impressed on you or an action step for you to take?

_____

_____

Pray Over the Week's "Take-away"...

Ask the Holy Spirit to embed the most significant thought or truth in your mind and spirit this coming week in a way that will help you consciously live in the shadow of that truth. Pray over any action step God has impressed on you.

Weeks Six to Eight

Getting Ready
Where We Have Been the Past Weeks...

What makes a man dangerous—dangerous in a good way? Is it a man's testosterone, love for adventure, innate willingness to risk and explore? What is it?

When we think of a man that is dangerous for good, what comes to your mind? Here are some qualities that come to my mind:

- Confident and secure because of who he is in Christ;
- Willing to risk whatever it takes to follow Christ wherever He leads us;
- Willing to do the right thing, regardless of personal cost;
- Courageous, even if it looks ridiculous to others;
- Passionate;
- Willing to follow Christ out of his comfort zone;
- Has a spirit of adventure;
- Willing to face life issues head-on;
- Rejects passivity flat-out;
- Understands that he is a partner with God;
- Treasures Christ in his heart above all else;
- Willing to be vulnerable;
- Can't help but be excited at what he sees God doing;
- Senses he may be in over his head, but is depending on God to come through.

Here's the reality: Most men are far more insecure than they like to admit. They go through their entire lives comparing and competing for their security and significance. As Joe Erhmann describes it, they go from the ball field to the bedroom to the billfold, always comparing themselves with others and measuring their worth.

John Eldredge said, "You are dangerous big-time. If you ever got your heart back, lived from it with courage, you would do a lot of damage—on the side of good."[1] As in the movie *Braveheart*, "All men die, few men live."

So, how does a man with a bent to insecurity from life-long comparing and competing get his heart back? How does he develop a genuine, real security and confidence that enables him to risk and dare and do the right thing when difficult and unpopular? Did God know what He was doing when He made man the way He did?

We have been looking for clues. We have been looking at the lives of dangerous men and asking, "What made them the way they are?" These are real men who have experienced real dangers of life and are impacting others for good.

We have also been looking in the Bible for God's thoughts. What if our security was rooted in how God longs for us to see ourselves—as His son? What if we grasped and felt the depth of our being loved by God forever and unconditionally? What if we knew without a doubt that we are accepted by God and are forever free from condemnation? What if we no longer compared, competed, and performed for our security and significance?

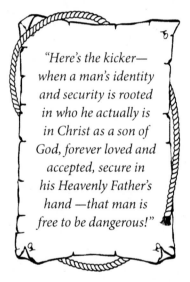

"*Here's the kicker— when a man's identity and security is rooted in who he actually is in Christ as a son of God, forever loved and accepted, secure in his Heavenly Father's hand —that man is free to be dangerous!*"

Here's the kicker—when a man's identity and security is rooted in who he actually is in Christ as a son of God, forever loved and accepted, secure in his Heavenly Father's hand—that man is free to be dangerous! He is free to step out and follow Christ wherever He may lead him. That man can live free and wild! Not reckless or stupid. He can live out the desires and passions that God puts in his heart.

Philip Yancey says two words would never apply to the Jesus of the Gospels—boring and predictable.[2] Jesus is always connecting with people in such a real way that something significant is always happening. Does the average man feel that his life is mostly boring, routine, and predictable? Probably. What if a man felt secure enough to follow Christ wherever He would lead him? Would that man experience life more as an adventure that demands the best of him? I think so!

How does a man develop a God-rooted identity in his heart? It definitely is a process of the Holy Spirit transforming our minds and spirit. This is why we have prioritized spending 10-15 minutes every day in an appointment with God.

"For the Word of God is living and active, sharper than any two-edged sword, piercing to the division of soul and of spirit, of joints and of marrow, and discerning the thoughts and intentions of the heart." –Hebrews 4:12, ESV

His Word through the Holy Spirit will find us—which is why you may have noticed a real battle comes when you plan a time to spend 10-15 minutes alone with God. The alarm won't go off, you'll feel you don't have time because of an important work project, etc. Our enemy will fight you as hard as he can on this front.

Here are a few ideas: Get alone with God in an extended way to cry out to Him over thoughts that He has impressed on you through your reading and times alone with Him. Go to a coffee shop or bookstore. Take turns taking care of the kids with your wife so each of you can find time to be alone with God. If you enjoy the outdoors, head for the mountains, a lake, a favorite park or trail, and listen with your heart to what He is saying to you. He will respond to the cry of your heart. You may need to get off the treadmill of our culture's pace to hear Him.

Where We Are Going the Next Several Weeks...

During weeks six through eight we will focus on how significant we are as God's workmanship, as His co-workers, and as the very salt and light of the world.

WEEK SIX

Game Plan

The Challenge

To see and appreciate the unique ways God has made us and is fashioning us now through the circumstances of life. Why has He made us the way He has and why have we experienced the circumstances we have? He is crafting us for the lifelong adventure of following Him—perhaps in ways we have never envisioned.

The Goal

To see ourselves as significant as God does—as His workmanship.

The Game Plan

Day 1

"Macaroni at Midnight" –Don Bartlette

Day 2

"The Pain of Loss" –Jerry White

Day 3

"The Question" –Henri Nouwen

Day 4

"The Test" –Louis Zamperini

Day 5

"A Most Unreasonable Assignment" –Bob Boardman

Day 6

"Reflection on Week Six"

My Appointment
with God

Best Time

Best Location

WEEK SIX

I am God's Workmanship
Day 1 - "Macaroni at Midnight"

A Story of a Dangerous Man

Don Bartlette was born into a dysfunctional family in North Dakota. He was born without an upper lip, had a large hole in the roof of his mouth, and half of his nose was hanging loose. The doctor looked at him and told his father, "Send him away." His father would not even look at him and took refuge in alcohol.

Officials initially refused to allow him to attend school. When he did attend, he was beaten and ridiculed by the students, tied up to a tree, spit on, and locked in the janitor's closet. He would go to a garbage dump where he found food, clothes, reading material, and his closest friends—the rats. Out of his hunger, he would pick up the food he found and push it down his throat. He had never learned to chew his food. During these years he was unable to speak.

Inside, Don thought, "If I had my father's knife, I would hurt my tormentors. If I had his rifle, I would eliminate their laughter." One time, he grabbed his father's rifle to shoot him, but his mother stopped him from pulling the trigger.

When he was about to become a teen, a wealthy woman moved by compassion took Don into her home. She taught him how to speak, chew his food, work for money, and she also opened the Bible to him. One night he excitedly ran home to his parents to show them he could speak. At midnight he said the word "macaroni" for his parents.

Don grew up and married a woman who followed Christ. She invited him to a church in Minnesota where the pastor spoke on Matthew 7:7 *"ask, seek, and knock."* The next day he pulled his car to the side of the road and asked Christ to come into his life. He felt the hate leave him as he experienced the arms of God surrounding him. Don is thankful for the woman who took him into her home, for his wife, and most thankful for Christ who loved him and died for him, teaching him to love all men.

Don graduated as valedictorian in his high school, earned a doctorate, and worked as a counselor. Today he is a sought-after speaker.[1]

Read Ephesians 2:10 and Psalm 139:13-16

Respond:

1. Do you think God is in control when each of us is formed in our mother's womb?

_____

_____

2. Why do you think God made us the way we are?

_____

_____

Your Story:

What gifts did God uniquely give you when He made you?

_____

_____

How are you using those gifts for the good of others?

_____

_____

WEEK SIX

I am God's Workmanship
Day 2 - "The Pain of Loss"

A Story of a Dangerous Man

Jerry White is the former president and chief executive officer of The Navigators, an international Christian organization that has its roots in the Navy in World War II. I first met Jerry when he was working toward his doctorate in aeronautical engineering at Purdue University. Since then he has worked in the space program, taught at the Air Force Academy, and become a general in the Air Force. He also has authored several books, including *Dangers Men Face*.

But something happened in April 1990, that neither Jerry nor his wife, Mary, had ever envisioned. Their 30-year-old son, Steve, was brutally murdered while driving a cab in Colorado Springs.

Their world was turned upside down. But through the process of grieving, Jerry's confidence in the goodness and sovereignty of God deepened. "Even more significant was the change in my identity as a man. Suddenly work and accomplishments meant almost nothing. My identity as a father, husband, friend, and frail human being emerged and deepened. My identity as a child of God took on new meaning."[1]

In the process of grieving his loss, Jerry grew in the lifelong process of shifting his identity from one based on accomplishments to one based on being a child of God.[2]

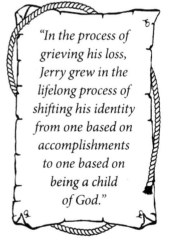

"In the process of grieving his loss, Jerry grew in the lifelong process of shifting his identity from one based on accomplishments to one based on being a child of God."

Read Isaiah 64:8 and Isaiah 45:9

Respond:

1. How is God described in these passages?

2. How is man described?

Your Story:

How do you see God fashioning and molding you these days?

How is He asking you to cooperate with Him?

WEEK SIX

I am God's Workmanship
Day 3 - "The Question"

A Story of a Dangerous Man

As **Henri Nouwen** entered his fifties, he asked himself the question: "Did becoming older bring me closer to Jesus?" After 25 years of living in the priesthood, he found himself praying poorly, living isolated from others, and being preoccupied with the culture's burning issues. Twenty of those years were spent teaching at the University of Notre Dame, Yale Divinity School, and Harvard. Yet something inside him was telling him that his success was putting his own soul at risk. He felt burned out, which for him was a convenient psychological explanation for his spiritual death. His heart was shrinking.[1]

In the midst of this he kept praying, "Lord, show me where you want me to go and I will follow You, but please be clear and unambiguous about it!" The answer came through Jean Vanier, founder of the L'Arche Communities for the mentally handicapped. God said, "Go and live among the poor in spirit, and they will heal you." So he moved from Harvard to L'Arche to be a priest to the mentally handicapped.[2]

This experience was the most important experience of his new life, because it forced him to rediscover his true identity. "These broken, wounded, and completely unpretentious people forced me to let go of my relevant self—the self that can do things, show things, prove things, build things—and forced me to reclaim that unadorned self in which I am completely vulnerable, open to receive and give love regardless of any accomplishments."[3]

> "The great message we have is that God loves us not because of what we do or accomplish, but because He created and reedeemed us in love."

He became deeply convinced that the Christian leader of the future is called to be in this world with nothing to offer but his own vulnerable self, just as Jesus did. The great message we have is that God loves us not because of what we do or accomplish, but because He created and redeemed us in love.[4]

Though this truth can sound simple and even trite, very few people know they are loved without any conditions or limits.[5]

Read John 21:15-19

Respond:

1. Why do you think Jesus asked Peter the same question three times: "Simon, son of John, do you love me?"

_____

_____

2. In your words, what do you think it means to "love Christ"?

_____

_____

Your Story:

It's possible to be very knowledgeable about Christ and active in church events and responsibilities, yet not deepening in our heart for God. How do you feel you are doing in knowing the heart of Christ and loving Him in the way you described above?

_____

_____

WEEK SIX

I am God's Workmanship
Day 4 - "The Test"

A Story of a Dangerous Man

Louie Zamperini was a world-class runner who competed on the US Olympic team in the 1936 Olympic games in Berlin. He wanted a Nazi flag for a souvenir, so he shinnied up a 50-foot flagpole and brought down the swastika, and was almost shot in the process!

After the Japanese attack on Pearl Harbor on December 7, 1941, Louie joined the Air Corps. He was shot down over the Pacific and survived 47 days on a life raft. Louie and the only other surviving crewmember ended up on the Japanese occupied island of Guam. They were immediately captured and sent to a prison camp in Japan.

In prison, Louie was brutally beaten and starved. Once, a notorious guard nicknamed "The Bird" by the Allied prisoners beat him 14 days in a row with his steel belt buckle, and then forced him to compete in running events. Louie had prayed to God for mercy and repented when on the life raft, and now while in prison he repented again. He returned home after the war as a hero and a heavy drinker. He forgot God and his promise to serve Him if his life was spared. His search for notoriety and wealth caused him to deny God.

> *"His biggest test was to return to his former prison, face his former guards and say, 'I forgive you, in Christ's name.'"*

Louie finally repented from his rebelliousness and returned to Japan for a few months to share the Gospel of Christ with the Japanese people. But his biggest test was to return to his former prison, face his former guards and say, "I forgive you, in Christ's name." By the grace of God, Louie was able to do this.

Louie told his story at a meeting in 1951, which was attended by a man named Bob Boardman. Bob was fighting God's calling to return to Japan as a missionary. The rest of this story is found in tomorrow's story of a dangerous man.[1]

Read Luke 23:32-35 and Matthew 18:21-35

Respond:

1. Why do you think Jesus asked the Father to forgive his tormentors?

2. When Peter asked Jesus how often he would be required to forgive an offender, Jesus answered with a story. How would you summarize the essence of Jesus' story?

Your Story:

Are you struggling with forgiving someone?

WEEK SIX

I am God's Workmanship
Day 5 - "A Most Unreasonable Assignment"

A Story of a Dangerous Man

I was sitting in a church in Kirkland, Washington, when my friend Jon whispered to me, "Have you met **Bob Boardman?**" I replied, "No, but I sure would like to." Jon proceeded to invite Bob to join us for dinner at Jon's home.

While having dinner, I was able to hear Bob's story first hand. World War II had marked him for life. Early in the war, during a drunken brawl, he had punched his hand through a store window, severing the tendons in his right hand. As a result, Bob found himself in an Australian hospital. While lying in that hospital he started reading his *Gideon's New Testament* daily and unashamedly. After three months of reading the New Testament, the love Christ had for him became real and drew Bob to committing his heart and life to Him.[1]

Two years later, Bob was fighting on Okinawa just four days before the end of combat on that island, in June of 1945. A Japanese sniper shot Bob through the neck, the bullet shattering his windpipe passing through his trigger finger. The agony of just trying to breathe made him feel as if he was drowning. He thought for sure he was dying.

Bob cried out to God for deliverance. About this time a buddy's tank appeared, and the tank crew spotted him, helped him into the tank, and drove on to find him medical help. Because of the events of that fateful day, Bob now always speaks in a hoarse whisper. He says he has "permanent laryngitis."

During his recovery, Bob prayed, "I'm willing to go anywhere in the world, except Japan." He could not accept what he thought was a very unreasonable assignment from God. But still he knew God was calling him to be a missionary to Japan. After hearing the story of Louie Zamperini (told earlier) at a meeting in 1951, Bob's resistance to the Lord broke down. On December 31, 1951, Bob and his wife Jean, went to Japan and spent most of the next 36 years working as missionaries to the people who were formerly his enemies.

Read Matthew 26:36-40, Hebrews 12:1-2, and Luke 9:23-25

Respond:

1. Describe what Jesus thought and how he felt at Gethsemane.

_____

_____

2. What motivated Jesus to willingly go through with dying on the cross?

_____

_____

Your Story:

Are you struggling with giving up your control in order to follow Christ in a way that seems unreasonable or hard?

_____

_____

What is He asking you to do?

_____

_____

Can you trust Him?

_____

_____

WEEK SIX

I am God's Workmanship
Day 6 - "Reflection on the Week"

Do you feel insignificant... too small to really make a difference? Do you ever think: "I can barely keep my head above water with my work, family, and church responsibilities. How could God use my life in a significant way?"

In fact, if you see yourself as small and dependent, you are exactly the kind of humble person God wants to use—and you qualify for God's grace.

"God opposes the proud but gives grace to the humble." –I Peter 5:5, ESV[1]

You are very significant in the eyes of God. We need to align our thinking and feelings with God's thinking!

"The least one shall become a clan, and the smallest one a mighty nation;
I am the Lord; in it's time I will hasten it." -Isaiah 60:22, ESV

God had you in His heart and mind before the world was made. Isaiah 49:16 says you are engraved in the palm of His hands. As we have seen in the stories of Don Bartlette, Jerry White, Henri Nouwen, Louie Zamperini, and Bob Boardman, He is the kind of God who carefully fashions us. He is working and crafting us through our experiences, pain, prayers, and availability.

To make ourselves available to God is one choice we alone can make; no one can make that choice for us. The apostle Paul says:

"I appeal to you therefore, brothers, by the mercies of God to present your
bodies as a living sacrifice." –Romans 12:1, ESV

God is asking you and I to freely offer our hearts, lives, and bodies to Him. He doesn't force or coerce us. He asks us.

Jack Hayford shared at a Promise Keepers Conference in 1994 that each morning after he awakes, he kneels beside his bed and offers himself to God as a living sacrifice to do whatever He wants. Since that event, each morning I pray a similar prayer of offering myself to Him to follow, love, and trust Him with my whole heart.

How long has it been since you told the Lord that you are totally available to Him for His purposes? Have you ever told Him? This is a good time to affirm your availability to Him in whatever way you choose. When you do, ask Him to help you see how He is fashioning you through your life circumstances, family background, people He has brought into your life, and especially your pain.

Remember to thank God for the way He is fashioning you for His unique purposes.

A Few Dangerous Questions...

Did it work for you this past week to make space in your life to connect with your Heavenly Father in a real way for 10-15 minutes a day, or most days?

If not, what changes do you need to make?

Was there a time during the past week when God impressed upon you to say or do something, but responding would have taken you out of your comfort zone?

How did you respond?

Reflect Over Your Journaling the Past Week...

What was the week's "take-away"—the most important truth God impressed on you or an action step for you to take?

Pray Over the Week's "Take-away"...

Ask the Holy Spirit to embed the most significant thought or truth in your mind and spirit this coming week in a way that will help you consciously live in the shadow of that truth. Pray over any action step God has impressed on you.

Week Seven

Game Plan

The Challenge

We live in a world that values the big, the spectacular, the up-front gifts used in large gatherings of people. If a large number of people are present, it is important and significant. If not, it doesn't matter. Then we may conclude, "God can't use me in a significant way because I don't have those gifts." But God is the God of "mustard seed" faith (Matthew 13:31-32) who loves to use what looks small and insignificant.

Our challenge is to believe Paul's words to the Corinthians:

"God chose what is foolish in the world to shame the wise... what is weak in the world to shame the strong... what is low and despised in the world... to bring to nothing the things that are." –I Corinthians 1:27-28, ESV[1]

Your challenge is to believe God wants to use your life in a significant way.

The Goal

To see ourselves as significant as God does—as His co-worker.

The Game Plan

Day 1

"Always Holding Someone Up" –Dawson Trotman

Day 2

"One Chance in Four Billion" –Hubert Mitchell

Day 3

"Extreme Risk-Taking" –Abraham

Day 4

"Believing Versus Following" –Jan Hettinga

Day 5

"The Delight of a Dangerous Man" –Jim Downing

Day 6

"Reflection on Week Seven"

My Appointment with God

Best Time

Best Location

Week Seven

I am God's Co-worker
Day 1 - "Always Holding Someone Up"

A Story of a Dangerous Man

On the afternoon of June 18, 1956, a speedboat skimmed across Schroon Lake in upstate New York. Swerving and turning into the wake for the fun of it, **Dawson Trotman** and his friends laughed and enjoyed the moment. Suddenly the boat made a fast right turn and smacked a wave, catapulting Dawson and one of the girls in the boat, a non-swimmer, into the lake. Daws gripped the girl's wrist, steadily holding her up, treading water until the boat came back for them. The girl was rescued. Daws sank and disappeared into the water.[1]

Time Magazine told the world about his death in its July 2, 1956 edition. Under his picture was the caption, "Always Holding Someone Up." The article started with, "So died Dawson Trotman, 'The Navigator,' light and power of a movement (The Navigators) that echoes the Words of the Scriptures around the world."[2]

Billy Graham said of him, "I think Dawson touched more lives than any man I have ever known."[3]

As a 20-year-old, Daws had been in trouble with the law and was plagued with drinking, gambling, and lying. After one scuffle with the law, he promised God that he would serve Him the rest of his life. The next Sunday evening he went to a church youth group. Two leaders of the group divided them into teams and challenged them to memorize ten verses the next week. The losing team was to treat the winning team to a picnic lunch.

Daws memorized all ten verses. Soon after, while walking to work, he reviewed John 5:24. Suddenly the truth of that verse struck home, and he paused and prayed to receive Christ into his life. He set himself the goal of memorizing a verse a day and reviewing systematically all he had learned earlier. In the first three years of his Christian life he memorized more than 1,000 verses.[4]

Daws spent time with God in the Bible daily and loved to claim His promises while praying with his friends in the hills and mountains of California. He began connecting with sailors and helped them grow in their walk with Christ. During World War II, the Navigators' prayer meetings and Bible studies multiplied to over 1,000 groups on ships and bases.[5]

Read Isaiah 58:6-12

Respond:

1. What promises is God making in verses 9-12?

_____

_____

2. What are the conditions, the "ifs" of God fulfilling His promises in the above verses?

_____

_____

Your Story:

Do you see yourself as one whom God can use to raise up the "foundations of many generations" (verse 12) of followers of Christ, beginning with your sons, sons-in-law, grandsons, and nephews?

_____

_____

Week Seven

I am God's Co-worker
Day 2 - "One Chance in Four Billion"

A Story of a Dangerous Man

As a teenager growing up in Chicago in the 1950's, I remember a man named **Hubert Mitchell**. He spoke at our church and played the accordion—how's that for going back in time! There was an authenticity about him that caused him to stand out. I've only recently learned the story about his life.

When the Japanese bombed Pearl Harbor and brought America into World War II, Hube Mitchell and his family were missionaries in Sumatra (now Indonesia) working with the primitive Kubu people. When he first explained the Gospel to the Kubus, they asked him, "What is a cross?"

He demonstrated his answer by cutting down two small trees and laying one across the other in the form of a cross. "How can a man die by lying upon the trunks of two trees?" they asked Hube. "Wicked men drove nails into the hands and feet of Jesus, and the blood left His body," Hube explained.

"What is a nail?" inquired the tribesmen, who had never before seen a nail. Hube and his co-workers searched but could not find a nail. "Please, Lord," he prayed, "give me some way to explain a nail to these people, so they can believe in Jesus."

One day after a lunch of rice and dried fish, the Kubus watched Hube take a can of mandarin oranges from his knapsack. The cans had been packed in Japan and bought at a Chinese store 100 miles from his base. He poured the oranges from the can into his tin dish. As he started to throw the can away, he heard a rattling sound. To his amazement he saw a shiny three-inch nail inside the can.

"Look," he shouted, "This is a nail—like the long ones used to nail Jesus to the cross!" (A mathematics professor calculated there was one chance in four billion that a nail would be in that particular can.) The people wept as they realized how much God loved them. Many responded to this Good News and a new community of Christians began.[1]

Read Matthew 17:14-21

Respond:

1. Why couldn't the disciples heal the man's epileptic son?

2. What do you think is most important—the amount of our faith or what we are putting our faith in?

Your Story:

Is there something that now looks impossible to you (or almost impossible), but that you believe God would want you to trust Him to do?

WEEK SEVEN

I am God's Co-worker
Day 3 - "Extreme Risk-Taking"

A Story of a Dangerous Man

The story of the life of **Abraham** is told in Genesis 12-25 and Hebrews 11:8–12, 17–19, in the Bible. Abraham was absolutely one of the greatest risk-takers ever. I cannot read the story of his risk-taking and following God by faith without being deeply moved in my spirit.

His story begins in Genesis 12 with God calling him to leave his home and his father's family to a land God would show him. God promises to bless him so extensively that every family of the earth would be blessed through him and his offspring!

How did Abraham respond to God's call to leave the familiar to go to an unknown destination?

"So Abram left, as the Lord told him." —Genesis 12:4

Do you think this took him out of his comfort zone? Probably!

But his greatest test was yet before him. In Genesis 22:1-2, God told Abraham to take his only son, Isacc, and go to the land of Moriah to offer him there as a burnt offering on one of the mountains that He would show him. How do you rationalize this request of God? This has to be the most unreasonable assignment ever! Why would God ask him to do such an outrageous, cruel thing? Does God really know what He's doing? How did Abraham, at the age of 75, respond to this most unreasonable assignment from God?

"So Abraham rose early in the morning... and took his son, Isaac."
–Genesis 22:3

How could he do this? Read on to discover why God would call him to take this extreme risk.

Read Genesis 22:1-19 and Hebrews 11:6, 8-12, 17-19

Respond:

1. Describe the risk Abraham took:

2. What do you think enabled Abraham to obey God? (Hebrews 11:17-19)

3. Why did God call Abraham to sacrifice his only son? (Genesis 22:12)

4. What do you think Abraham learned from this experience? (Genesis 22:14)

Your Story:

What is God calling you to do that will take you out of your comfort zone and cause you to take risks (even extreme risks) to obey Him?

What will enable you to be faithful to follow and obey Him?

WEEK SEVEN

I am God's Co-worker
Day 4 - "Believing Versus Following"

A Story of a Dangerous Man

Jan Hettinga is pastor of Northshore Baptist Church in Kirkland, Washington, a church of 3,000 attendees. Under Jan's leadership, this church has planted five daughter churches, which in turn have planted five churches with a total of 2,000 attendees. I first heard of Jan in 1979, after my wife and I moved to Green Bay, Wisconsin. He was senior pastor at Bethel Baptist Church where we attended. After a week or two of our attending, he announced he was leaving to pastor a church in the Seattle, Washington area.

After leaving Wisconsin, Jan observed that only six to seven percent of those who professed Christ in his ministry and the evangelical world at large became productive transformed Christians over the long haul. This reality so disheartened Jan that he nearly quit the ministry, believing there must be something wrong with him. The fallout of lasting fruit in his ministry haunted him.

In desperation, he began to read the New Testament and set aside his perceptions of what ministry was and even what the Gospel was. It dawned on him that the problem with frustrating results in his ministry was a misunderstanding of the Gospel itself! What shook him was that not only had he been off-target, but most of the evangelical world was as well. He noticed that Jesus was always talking about the kingdom of God. What was this all about?

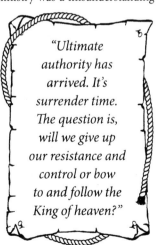

"*Ultimate authority has arrived. It's surrender time. The question is, will we give up our resistance and control or bow to and follow the King of heaven?*"

It became obvious to Jan that in our attempts to simplify the Gospel for mass consumption, the message of the Gospel was changed. He and his evangelical colleagues usually invited people to become Christians with phrases like, "Receive the gift of eternal life" and "Accept the pardon from sin paid for at the cross." What became glaringly obvious was that the Gospel of Jesus was clearly different from these phrases. Jesus consistently called His message the Gospel of the kingdom and He asked people to repent.

More than the acknowledgement of the truth that Jesus died for us (which is incredibly significant), repentance belongs with God's kingdom. Ultimate authority has arrived. It's surrender time. The question is, will we give up our resistance and control or bow to and follow the King of heaven?

Jesus referred to "the Gospel of the kingdom" because He was offering leadership and asking for followership. There are two kinds of "believing"—one in the sense of agreeing with the truth, and another in the sense of repentance and gladly following our Lord's leadership.[1]

Read Mark 10:17-30

Respond:

1. What was the control issue this wealthy young man faced?

_____

_____

2. How did Jesus communicate the Gospel to him?

_____

_____

Note Jesus' promise:

> "You will have treasure in heaven," and His invitation, "Come, follow Me."

Your Story:

What form of "wealth" do you have that you treasure that makes it difficult for you to follow Christ?

_____

_____

WEEK SEVEN

I am God's Co-worker
Day 5 "The Delight of a Dangerous Man"

A Story of a Dangerous Man

Jim Downing is one of the most amazing, dangerous (in a good way) men I have ever met! He enlisted in the U.S. Navy after graduating from high school in 1932. Jim survived the sinking of the battleship USS WEST VIRGINIA when it was torpedoed and bombed at Pearl Harbor on December 7, 1941. He established the Navigators ministry on that ship, working with sailors one-on-one and in small groups.

As Jim's Navy career of 24 years was winding down, Dawson Trotman urged him to join The Navigators staff full time. He traveled to Schroon Lake in upstate New York in 1956, to see Daws and accept his invitation. When he arrived, he found that Daws had drowned just a few hours earlier.[1]

One Friday evening in January 2002, at the age of 89, Jim traveled to our home prior to a speaking engagement the next morning. Before he arrived at our home, I wondered, "Would I have to help him get from his car to our house?" I discovered he was fully able to get from his car to our front door without my help!

Before calling it a night, we had a chance to catch up. Thirty years earlier I had listened to Jim speak on his favorite topics: "*Experiencing the Life of Christ by Meditating on God's Word*" and "*How to Have Communion with God.*" What he shared back then impacted me forever!

Here's what I will never forget about our time: He is a man 89 years old, and his heart for God is stronger than ever. Ministering to college students around the country energizes him! He still dreams and envisions projects that will extend God's kingdom reign in the hearts of people. (One project he has pursued is getting a New Testament in the hands of every 12-year-old in the country, since research has shown that children at this age are most receptive to hearing about Christ).

Since that time I have been asking God, "Lord, help me maximize my energy to follow you and your dreams and purposes for my life all the days of my life—even until I'm 89, like your servant Jim Downing."

Read Psalm 1 and Jeremiah 17:7-8

Respond:

1. Describe the delight of a blessed man (verses 1-2).

_____

_____

2. In what way is such a man like a nourished, fruitful tree?

_____

_____

Your Story:

Do you have any plan in place to grow your delight in God's Word by reading and/or memorizing and meditating on key verses of the Bible?

_____

_____

If so, what is your plan?

_____

_____

WEEK SEVEN

I am God's Co-worker
Day 6 · "Reflection on the Week"

A Brief Glance at the Week:

Day 1 – "Always Holding Someone Up" –Dawson Trotman
Day 2 – "One Chance in Four Billion" –Hubert Mitchell
Day 3 – "Extreme Risk-Taking" –Abraham
Day 4 – "Believing Versus Following" –Jan Hettinga
Day 5 – "The Delight of a Dangerous Man" –Jim Downing

A Few Questions As You Look Back at the Week...

Which story most impressed you? What passage of Scripture did God begin to write on your heart?

What do you think of Abraham's willingness to offer his only son because God asked him? What can we learn from his story?

"For whatever was written in former days was written
for our instruction that through endurance and through the
encouragement of the Scriptures we might have hope." –Romans 15:4, ESV

We can be confident that Abraham's story was written with you and me in mind—for our instruction, endurance, encouragement, and hope.

Dallas Willard said with his characteristically wry humor, "What is God's address? God's address is the end of your rope!" This is the same spirit of Matthew 5:3:

"You're blessed when you're at the end of your rope. With less of you there
is more of God and his rule." –The Message

Abraham had to feel at the end of his rope. We can imagine what he was thinking, "What? Sacrifice my only son? What in the world are You asking me to do?"

God knew what He was doing. Genesis 22:12 expresses what He was up to:

"...now I know that you fear God, seeing you have not withheld your son, your only son, from me." –Genesis 22:12, ESV

A.W. Tozer points out that Abraham was old when Isaac was born—old enough to be his grandfather! The child became the delight and idol of his heart. This is not hard to understand. The child represented everything sacred to his father's heart—the promises of God, the covenants, the hopes of the years, and the messianic dream. As he watched Isaac grow, Abraham's heart bonded ever so closely with his son—until the relationship began to compete with God Himself. It was then that God stepped in.[1]

At the last possible moment, God stopped him from slaying his son. It was as if God was saying, "It's okay, Abraham, I never intended that you should slay your son. I only wanted to remove him from the temple of your heart that I might reign unchallenged there. I wanted to correct the perversion that existed in your love."[2]

If you and I are serious about following and treasuring Christ in our hearts above all else, God will eventually test us in a similar way. He will go after the things that rival our treasuring Christ above everything and everyone else.[3]

A Prayer You Can Pray...

"Father, I want to know You and follow You, but my cowardly heart fears to give up its toys. I cannot part with them without inward bleeding. Please root from my heart the love of all those things that I have cherished so long, so that You may enter and live there without a rival.

–In Jesus' name, Amen."[4]

A Few Dangerous Questions...

Did it work for you this past week to make space in your life to connect with your Heavenly Father in a real way for 10-15 minutes a day, or most days?

_____

_____

If not, what changes do you need to make?

_____

_____

Was there a time during the past week when God impressed upon you to say or do something, but responding would have taken you out of your comfort zone?

_____

_____

How did you respond?

_____

_____

Reflect Over Your Journaling the Past Week...

What was the week's "take-away"—the most important truth God impressed on you or an action step for you to take?

_____

_____

Pray Over the Week's "Take-away"...

Ask the Holy Spirit to embed the most significant thought or truth in your mind and spirit this coming week in a way that will help you consciously live in the shadow of that truth. Pray over any action step God has impressed on you.

WEEK EIGHT

Game Plan

The Challenge

"You are the salt of the earth." –Matthew 5:13, ESV

"Let me tell you why you are here. You're here to be salt-seasoning that brings out the God-flavors of this earth." –Matthew 5:13, The Message

"You are the light of the world." –Matthew 5:14, ESV

"You're here to be light, bringing out the God-colors in the world."
–Matthew 5:16, The Message

Do you see yourself as significant? God does. He says you are the very salt of the world. Without salt, food can either rot or lose its flavor. Without God, people self-destruct and live flat, insipid lives shot through with futility.

Not only are you the salt of the world, you are the light by which people desperately need to live. Without it, they live in darkness. It's no fun to live in darkness, not being able to see. People without light get bruised and broken by life's blows, and lose hope.

Practically speaking, how does one actually be salt and light to people? First, a warning: Don't just rely on bringing your neighbors and friends to your church to expose them to the light of the Gospel. Some will come. Many will not. It has been documented that many men are not attracted to our churches. They see it as a "women's thing."[1]

As Scott Morton points out in *Down to Earth Discipling*, you have a very powerful secret resource. What is it? He gives us a clue from a speech by Colin Powell. He pleaded with the people to whom he was speaking to help economically deprived young people, but warned them, "It's more than just throwing computers at them." Powell went on to explain that organizing programs is not enough. He asked them to **spend quality time with youngsters–to give them personal attention one by one.**[2]

Colin Powell understands that programs alone cannot bring lasting change. There are a huge number of quality Christian programs in the U.S., but we are not penetrating the culture on a broad scale with the Gospel.

When personal attentiveness is added to a program, the impact can be powerful. Read the stories this week to see vivid illustrations of God blessing men who are willing to take risks and who respond to initiatives prompted by the Holy Spirit.[3]

The Goal

To see ourselves as significant as God does—as being salt and light to those in your relational world.

The Game Plan

Day 1

"Quiet Risk-Taking" –Edward Kimball

Day 2

"The Impact of Quiet Risk-Taking" –Dwight Moody

Day 3

"He Died Looking Me Straight in the Eyes" –LeRoy Eims

Day 4

"No Reserves, No Retreats, No Regrets" –William Borden

Day 5

"The Insider" –Jim Petersen

Day 6

"Reflection on Week Eight"

My Appointment with God

Best Time

Best Location

Week Eight

I am the Salt and Light of the World
Day 1 - "Quiet Risk-taking"

A Story of a Dangerous Man

Have you ever heard of **Edward Kimball**? —Probably not. He was a Sunday school teacher for young working men in Boston in the 1850's. On Saturday morning, April 21, 1855, Kimball left his lodging for Holton's Shoe Store. God had prompted him to speak to one of his students, Dwight Moody, who was working as a shoe clerk in the store.

Kimball was concerned that the other clerks would think he was trying to make a good boy out of him. He was so deep in his worries that at first he passed right by the shoe store. Then he decided to go back and quickly get it over with.

Kimball found the shoe clerk in the back of the store. There were tears in his eyes as he told the young man about Christ. Kimball later looked back and thought he communicated poorly, but the young shoe clerk responded within the hour by receiving Christ into his heart!

Not too many remember the name of Edward Kimball. But many have heard of the shoe clerk—Dwight Moody! God blessed Kimball's quiet risk-taking and response to the Holy Spirit's prompting. Tomorrow's story about Dwight Moody will reveal how God blessed him and used him powerfully in the lives of people around the world.[1]

"It was the church's program plus the personal attentiveness of one man that the Holy Spirit used to powerfully impact Dwight Moody—and then, thousands of others more."

It was the church's program plus the personal attentiveness of one man that the Holy Spirit used to powerfully impact Dwight Moody—and then, thousands of others more.

Read Galatians 5:16-17, 22-23 and II Chronicles 16:9

Respond:

1. What do you think it means to "walk by the Spirit"?

2. When a man responds to the Holy Spirit's prompting to step out of his comfort zone, how does God respond to that man?

Your Story:

How has the Holy Spirit been prompting you that takes you out of your comfort zone?

How have you been responding?

Week Eight

I am the Salt and Light of the World
Day 2 - "The Impact of Quiet Risk-taking"

A Story of a Dangerous Man

Dwight L. Moody was a poor, uneducated farm boy whose dad died when he was four. As a teen he went to Boston to sell shoes in his uncle's store. He attended church only because his uncle made him.

A visit by his Sunday school teacher, Edward Kimball, resulted in Dwight embracing Christ with his heart—as told in yesterday's story. Dwight was excited about his newfound faith and couldn't keep it to himself. His appetite for the Bible caused him to read and study God's Word, and each week he would share what he learned at his church's prayer meetings. But these educated people did not take to his poor grammar, his stories, and his loudness. Since he didn't feel accepted, he left Boston and went to Chicago.

His success in selling shoes there motivated him to set a goal of making $100,000—a huge amount in the 1850's. Meanwhile, he went to a mission in the poorest part of Chicago to invite them to his Sunday school class. His Sunday school grew from twelve students to fifteen hundred! During this time of explosive growth, one of his Sunday school teachers was dying and asked Dwight to come with him to invite each of the girls in his class to receive Christ. After seeing each girl receive Christ that night, he no longer cared about selling shoes and making a lot of money. His passion was to reach Chicago for Christ.

He became well known and started speaking in cities throughout the United States, England, and Scotland. He started the Moody Bible Institute in Chicago to train Christian workers. This school has sent more than 6,000 missionaries to other countries. More than 100 million people have heard or read the Gospel through Dwight Moody's work.[1]

Students attending the Moody Bible Institute are given an assignment in the Chicago area—a practical opportunity to share Christ or help others mature in

> *"After seeing each girl receive Christ that night, he no longer cared about selling shoes and making a lot of money. His passion was to reach Chicago for Christ."*

Christ. In 1956, two Moody students were assigned to be counselors to Fenger High School's HI-C Club, similar to Young Life and Youth for Christ clubs. That year one of the girls in Fenger's Hi-C Club approached one of the Moody students with the question, "How does one become a member of one's church?" The counselor proceeded to help her realize that what mattered most was having a personal relationship with Christ. The girl's name was Shirlee Spoolstra, who invited Christ into her life that day—and became my wife seven years later.

Do you think Edward Kimball had any idea of how God was going to bless his conversation with a shoe clerk by the name of Dwight Moody in the back of a shoe store?

Read Ezekiel 22:30 and II Timothy 3:14-17
Respond:

1. Describe the kind of man God is looking for.

_____

_____

2. How does God use the Scriptures to equip a man for the good works planned for him?

_____

_____

Your Story:

What do you think you need to do to be ready for all God has planned for you?

_____

_____

WEEK EIGHT

I am the Salt and Light of the World
Day 3 - "He Died Looking Me Straight in the Eyes"

A Story of a Dangerous Man

LeRoy Eims was a 19-year-old machine gunner on a tank when on September 15, 1944, the First Marine Division attacked Peleliu Island. Hidden in this tiny island were 10,000 dug-in Japanese soldiers, waiting for the American Marines to attack.

And attack they did! LeRoy was in zero wave. The only ones in front of him were the enemy. His tank got stuck on the coral surrounding the island, and became a sitting duck. Total bedlam was unleashed. LeRoy races for cover. A Marine lay by him in a pool of blood after being riddled by machine gun bullets. The wounded Marine grabs Eims: "Mate, I need help. Do you know how to pray?"

"Pray? I didn't know how to pray. I grabbed a fellow crawling by us, and asked, 'Do you know how to pray?' He cussed me out, so I figured I had the wrong guy. When I turned back to the wounded man, **he died looking me right straight in the eyes**."

LeRoy never forgot that man's look. He wondered where that dead Marine went when he died. He didn't know, but he was going to find out. He had to know the answer.

After the war, LeRoy went back to his home in Council Bluffs, Iowa, to work for the railroad. While working in nearby Harlan, IA on a Sunday morning he and his wife Virginia heard church bells ringing and decided to go to church. After the service, people greeted them and invited them to a church party and afterward to their homes for dinner. He was taken in by their love and warmth and noticed they all had Bibles in their homes.

He bought a big, black Holy Bible for $24.50 from a Bible salesman and brought it to work each day. He would complete his required work within 30 minutes and then was free to read the Bible for seven and a half hours a day. He discovered that God really loved him, and that Jesus died for his sins. LeRoy was deeply impacted by his discovery and gave his life to Christ.[1]

I have two vivid memories of LeRoy Eims. The first was when I was a graduate student at the University of Illinois and LeRoy came to speak at an ice cream social where we brought two friends to hear about Christ. Immediately after hearing LeRoy, my wife Shirlee and I went to the hospital where Shirlee gave birth to our son Scott on February 18, 1966.

The second memory was hearing LeRoy speak on "*How to Keep the Joybells Ringing*" at our first Navigators Staff Conference in 1971. He shared the pain of having a son who rejected Christ to live a life of drugs, thievery, and who was in a maximum-security prison for the rest of his life. He also shared how God gave him grace. He urged us to memorize a dozen verses on the love of God and the sovereignty of God. LeRoy's example and encouragement helped me weather future tempests in my life that I never imagined at the time.

Read II Chronicles 20:1-23

Respond:

What enabled Jehoshaphat to be victorious in battle?

_____

_____

Your Story:

What will enable you to be victorious in your life battles?

_____

_____

WEEK EIGHT

I am the Salt and Light of the World
Day 4 - "No Reserves, No Retreats, No Regrets"

A Story of a Dangerous Man

As heir to the Borden Dairy Estate, **William Borden** graduated as a millionaire from a Chicago high school in 1904. His parents gave him a trip around the world as a graduation present. As he traveled through Asia, the Middle East, and Europe, he felt a deep burden for the hurting people. He wrote home to say, "I'm going to give my life to prepare for the mission field." After this decision, he wrote in his Bible: **"No Reserves."**[1]

Borden arrived at Yale University in 1905. One of his friends noticed, "He came to college far ahead spiritually, of any of us. He had already given his heart in full surrender to Christ…" He started a movement at Yale. He would meet with one to three friends to pray and read the Bible. He would note any promises and then claim them in prayer. By the time Borden was a senior, one thousand of Yale's 1,300 students were meeting in such groups. Upon graduation from Yale, he turned down some high paying job offers. He also wrote two more words in his Bible: **"No Retreats."**

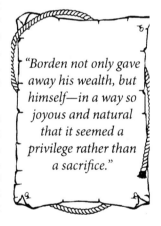

"Borden not only gave away his wealth, but himself—in a way so joyous and natural that it seemed a privilege rather than a sacrifice."

After graduate work at Princeton Seminary, he sailed for China. Because of his heart to work with Muslims, he stopped first in Egypt to study Arabic. While there, he contracted spinal meningitis. Within a month, 25-year-old William Borden was dead. "Borden not only gave away his wealth, but himself—in a way so joyous and natural that it seemed a privilege rather than a sacrifice."[2]

Prior to his death, Borden had written two more words in his Bible. Underneath the words "No Reserves" and "No Retreats," he had written: **"No Regrets."**[3]

Read Matthew 9:36-38, and Mark 10:17-22

Respond:

1. How would you describe Jesus' heart for people?

_____

_____

2. How did Jesus feel about the rich young man in Mark 10:21?

_____

_____

Your Story:

How would you describe your heart for people?

_____

_____

WEEK EIGHT

I am the Salt and Light of the World
Day 5 - "The Insider"

A Story of a Dangerous Man

Jim Petersen grew up in a Christian home in St. James, Minnesota, and graduated from the University of Minnesota. When he was 21 years old, God became the most important influence in his life and Jim began a consuming search to know Him personally. This search led him to Ed Reis, a Navigator representative, for mentoring in his relationship with Christ.[1]

Jim and his wife Marge moved to Brazil in August of 1963, to work as Navigator missionaries. For the next ten years they invested fruitfully in Brazilian university students and young professionals. These young people had largely abandoned their religious tradition to embrace secular philosophies. During this time Jim's thinking about sharing the Gospel was turned upside down. When he communicated the Bridge Illustration, an effective tool for communicating the Gospel in the U.S., their response was, "You came all the way here just to tell us this?" Jim knew he had to change his approach with those who had no biblical or Christian heritage.

Jim and his little team of missionary friends from the United States did life together with the students and young professionals. But the key thing they did was read and interact over the Bible together, especially the Gospel of John. Over time, one person after another was irresistibly attracted to Christ and gave their lives to Him.

Jim is driven by this truth: Almost half of our society is unchurched, and we Christians are not communicating with them very well. Many of the people in that half will not come to us or to our programs, but they are still reachable. We need to learn to bring Christ to them on their own turf.[2]

"Due to our busy lifestyles, fears, and inadequacies, we can fail to see God's heart and design for those around us."

The thing Jim and Marge most enjoy doing together is opening up the message of Christ to friends who have never taken a serious look at Him before. This passion and joy has led Jim to write *The Insider*. This book is a powerful encouragement to see that God's calling and purposes for us are to be worked out within our existing relational networks where we are already positioned as insiders. We're part of it—our families, neighborhoods, and workplaces.[3] But due to our busy lifestyles, fears, and inadequacies, we can fail to see God's heart and design for those around us. We miss cooperating with Him in His eternal purposes for them. Jim's encouragement helps us see that we can do it!

Read John 17:1-26

Respond:

1. Who did Jesus connect with relationally (verse 6)?

_____

_____

2. What did Jesus do with people the Father brought into His life?

In verse 8:

_____

In verse 9:

_____

In verse 11:

_____

In verse 18:

_____

3. Why did Jesus do what He did with people the Father brought into His life? (verse 23)

_____

_____

Your Story:

Name a person (or persons) who God has brought into your life with whom you sense an affinity.

_____

_____

What is one way you could love and serve them?

_____

_____

Week Eight

I am the Salt and Light of the World
Day 6 - "Reflection on the Week"

A Brief Glance at the Week:

Day 1 – "Quiet Risk-Taking" –Edward Kimball

Day 2 – "The Impact of Quiet Risk-Taking" –Dwight Moody

Day 3 – "He Died Looking Me Straight in the Eyes" –LeRoy Eims

Day 4 – "No Reserves, No Retreats, No Regrets" –William Borden

Day 5 – "The Insider" –Jim Petersen

A Few Questions as You Look Back at the Week...

1. Which story most impressed you?

_____

_____

2. What passage of Scripture did God begin to impress on your heart?

_____

_____

3. Do you see any trends—any threads of thought that God seems to be continually impressing on you?

_____

_____

4. Are you seeing yourself as increasingly significant as you see how much God wants to use you in the lives of your friends?

_____

_____

5. If so, how is your thinking changing as to how you see yourself?

_____

_____

Danger to Consider...

The question will come to mind… "If I limit my involvement with programs in order to focus on a few people God brings into my life, will I really feel fulfilled?"

In order to have space in your life to connect with other friends and neighbors, you must make choices to limit your involvement in other, good programs. You will risk rejection and misunderstanding, as you say no to other opportunities.

Albert Einstein is known to have had the following sign hanging in his office when he was at Princeton:

> **"Not everything that can be counted counts,
> and not everything that counts can be counted."**[1]

We can measure numbers of people who show up for events. We can measure other external behavioral changes. But if we're after transformation of people's hearts through the Holy Spirit's work, this can be a lot tougher to measure. Having people over for dinner, being available to talk over the fence, and crossing the street—these things take time and may never be noticed by other Christians. It takes patience, but we will see the effects in people's lives a little at a time, day-by-day, week-by-week.

Scott Morton, in his book *Down to Earth Discipling*, quotes this poem by an anonymous author:

> "Father, where shall I work today?
>> And my love flowed warm and free.
> Then He pointed out a tiny spot,
>> And said, 'Tend that for Me.'
> I answered quickly, 'Oh no, not that.
>> Why no one would ever see,
> No matter how well my work was done,
>> Not that little place for me!'
> And the word He spoke, it was not stern,
>> He answered me tenderly,
> 'Ah little one, search that heart of thine;
>> Art thou working for them or Me?
> Nazareth was a little place,
>> And so was Galilee." [2]

This poem reminds me that position and praise are not the goals. Einstein's quote helps me remember that what counts with God may not be counted by others.

A Few Dangerous Questions...

Did it work for you this past week to make space in your life to connect with your Heavenly Father in a real way for 10-15 minutes a day, or most days?

_____

_____

If not, what changes do you need to make?

_____

_____

Was there a time during the past week when God impressed upon you to say or do something, but responding would have taken you out of your comfort zone?

_____

_____

How did you respond?

_____

_____

Reflect Over Your Journaling the Past Week...

What was the week's "take-away"—the most important truth God impressed on you or an action step for you to take?

_____

_____

Pray Over the Week's "Take-away"...

Ask the Holy Spirit to embed the most significant thought or truth in your mind and spirit this coming week in a way that will help you consciously live in the shadow of that truth. Pray over any action step God has impressed on you.

THE MOST DANGEROUS MAN WHO EVER LIVED

Who would you vote for as the most dangerous man for good that ever lived? I would vote for Jesus Christ, hands-down. Here's why:

He did more damage for good than any man who ever lived. He totally trashed the enemy's (Satan) kingdom.

> "...that through death he might destroy the one who has the power of death, that is, the devil, and deliver all those who through fear of death were subject to lifelong slavery." –Hebrews 2:14–15, ESV

> "He disarmed the rulers and authorities and put them in open shame, by triumphing over them in him." –Colossians 2:15, ESV

He lived His whole life in danger. As a baby, He had to flee to Egypt with His parents because of Herod's search and destroy mission targeting Him (Matthew 2:13). He constantly did good, healing the sick and the lame, with those seeking to kill Him looking over His shoulder (John 5:18, 7:1,19,25). Jesus' claim to be the Son of God constituted a huge threat to the religious authorities of the time. What was their response to being threatened? Stone Him! (John 8:59, 9:31) His detractors were continually seeking to arrest Him (John 10:39), and His life ended in a violent death.

Peter described Jesus' suffering as an eyewitness:

> "...He suffered everything that came his way so you would know that it could be done, and also know how to do it, step-by-step. He never did one thing wrong, not once said anything amiss. They called him every name in the book and he said nothing back. He suffered in silence, content to let God set things right. He used his servant body to carry our sins to the cross so we could be rid of sin, free to live the right way. His wounds became your healing. You were lost sheep with no idea who you were or where you were going. Now you're named and kept for good by the Shepherd of your souls."
> –I Peter 2:21-25, The Message

What enabled Him to do this? He knew who He was—the beloved Son of His Heavenly Father and the object of His Father's pleasure (Matthew 3:17).

He knew where He came from and where He was going (John 8:14). What do you think enabled Him to go through with His mission of suffering, death, and love? He knew He could have opted out of the suffering (Matthew 26:38-40). His almighty Heavenly Father could have delivered Him from the violent death. He was committed at the core of His being to doing his Father's will and desire.

"...who for the joy that was set before him endured the cross, despising the shame, and is seated at the right hand of the throne of God."
–Hebrews 12:2, ESV

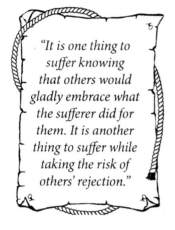

"It is one thing to suffer knowing that others would gladly embrace what the sufferer did for them. It is another thing to suffer while taking the risk of others' rejection."

He was looking forward to a lot of joy!

In His leaving the Father's presence and taking the form of a human being to suffer and die, He took the ultimate risk. It was the risk of our response. Would we blow Him off and live our lives with ourselves as our center? Or would we take Him seriously and embrace Him with our hearts as our Leader as well as Savior?

It is one thing to suffer knowing that others would gladly embrace what the sufferer did for them. It is another thing to suffer while taking the risk of others' rejection. Jesus could have used all the raw power at His disposal to force His will on His subjects, like others with power. But He didn't. He took the risk of our willing response. That, I will never understand, but His risk causes me to want to follow Him all the more with my heart.

"This is the kind of life you've been invited into, the kind of life Christ lived."
–I Peter 2:2, The Message

WEEK NINE

Key Learnings
What I Have Learned From Doing
The Making of a Dangerous Man

Below are the questions you answered as you began *The Making of a Dangerous Man*. To assess your progress up to now, once again answer each question using a number from 1 to 10, with 1 being the least true and 10 being the most true:

1. I am prone to play it safe when it comes to following Christ. ___
2. I feel very fulfilled in my life. ___
3. Life to me is an adventure I relish. ___
4. I can see God working in and through my daily relationships. ___
5. As a man, I feel secure and significant. ___
6. I enjoy reading the Bible, usually daily, and find it very relevant to my life. ___
7. I feel confident in conversing about my faith with unbelievers. ___
8. I feel busy and like I am operating on fumes. Often I feel hollow, shallow, and enslaved to a schedule that never lets up. ___
9. I find myself wanting to control my life and am very hesitant to follow and trust the leadership of Christ in real life. ___
10. I feel like I've found a cause that makes me come alive and is bringing out the best in me. ___

How would you describe your identity now?

_____

_____

Where do you get your security and significance?

_____

_____

How important to your identity is what you own, what you do (job title), and what others think of you?

_____

_____

WEEK NINE

Key Learnings

The past weeks we have focused on:

Weeks 3-5 – A Dangerous Man is Secure in Christ

Week Three – I am God's Son

Week Four – I am Loved By God · Forever and Unconditionally

Week Five – I am Accepted and Secure

Weeks 6-8 – A Dangerous Man is Significant in Christ

Week Six · I am God's Workmanship

Week Seven – I am God's Co-worker

Week Eight – I am the Salt and Light of the World

A Few Evaluative Questions to Identify Changes and Growth...

1. As you compare your responses to the questions at the beginning of *The Making of a Dangerous Man* with your responses now, what changes do you observe?

_____

_____

2. How has your identity changed as a result of focusing on the realities of who you are in Christ as noted above in weeks three to eight?

_____

_____

3. As you reflect over the past weeks, what were your key learnings from doing *The Making of a Dangerous Man*?

_____

_____

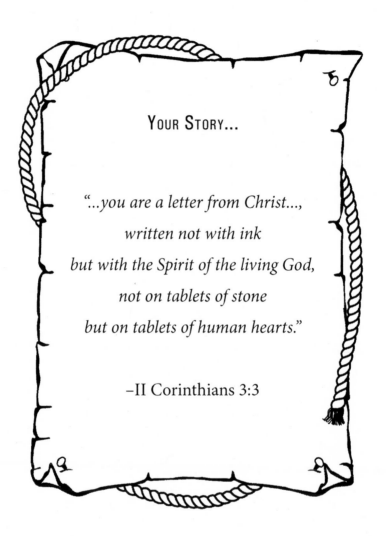

YOUR STORY...

"...you are a letter from Christ...,
written not with ink
but with the Spirit of the living God,
not on tablets of stone
but on tablets of human hearts."

–II Corinthians 3:3

Week Ten

Your Story
Turning Points

You have a unique history. In the midst of the events of your life, God is authoring your story. In the construct below, identify the major events in your life that were turning points. As a result of such significant milestones in your life, life was different changed for you in one or more areas of your life—your personal life, family, vocation, and relationships with other believers or unbelievers.

In the column "Impact On My Life," identify the major way or ways your life was impacted by each event. Ask God for the capacity to connect the dots between the events of your life and His purposes in those events. Look to and trust the Holy Spirit to guide your thinking.

AGE	TURNING POINTS	IMPACT ON MY LIFE

Note of Credit: This construct is similar to that included in the *LifePlan* material written, designed, and developed by Tom Paterson. Tom is the founder of the PathFinders Association, an association that facilitates one-on-one *LifePlans*. He has written a book, *Living The Life You Were Meant To Live*, which captures the *LifePlan* process. [1]

WEEK TEN

Your Story
Key Learnings

Identify key learnings from your turning points and their impact on your life:

_____

_____

_____

_____

_____

_____

In view of what God is currently doing in your life, what is one life area on which it would be wise to focus? This could be your personal/spiritual life, family, vocation, relationships with other believers, and relationships with other unbelievers. To cooperate with God in this area, identify the life area, a goal, and action plan:

Life area:

_____

Goal:

_____

Action plan:

_____

Will the above involve your taking risks and trusting God in new ways?

_____

_____

"Do you know why I often ask Christians, 'What's the biggest thing you've asked God for this week?' I remind them that they are going to God, the Father, and the Maker of the universe. The One who holds the world in His hands. What did you ask God for? Did you ask for peanuts, toys, trinkets, or did you ask for continents?

I want to tell you… it's tragic!

The little itsy-bitsy things we ask of our Almighty God. Sure, nothing is too small—but also nothing is too big. Let's learn to ask from our big God some of those big things He talks about.

"Call unto Me and I will answer thee,
and show thee great and mighty things
that thou knowest not." –Jeremiah 33:3, KJV[1]

–Dawson Trotman
Founder, The Navigators

Prayer Journal

*"Call to Me and I will answer you, and will tell you
great and hidden things that you have not known."*

–Jeremiah 33:3, ESV

Date	Requested by	Request	God's answer

Prayer Journal

*"Call to Me and I will answer you, and will tell you
great and hidden things that you have not known."*

–Jeremiah 33:3, ESV

Date	Requested by	Request	God's answer

Prayer Journal

*"Call to Me and I will answer you, and will tell you
great and hidden things that you have not known."*

–Jeremiah 33:3, ESV

Date	Requested by	Request	God's answer

Prayer Journal

"Call to Me and I will answer you, and will tell you
great and hidden things that you have not known."

–Jeremiah 33:3, ESV

Date	Requested by	Request	God's answer

Leader's Guide

If You Choose to Do
"The Making of a Dangerous Man"
with Other Men

Goals of "There's Danger Ahead" and "Getting Ready"

1. To connect with each other;

2. To realize and interact over the greatest dangers a man faces;

3. To have a basic idea of what it means to be dangerous from the example of the apostle Paul and also from people who have impacted us for good and for bad;

4. To see the potential benefits of doing *The Making of a Dangerous Man* with other men over the coming weeks;

5. To count the cost (Luke 14:28-30) of doing *The Making of a Dangerous Man* and determine willingness to pay the price;

6. To plan the best time and place for one's appointment with God.

Note: It may take three weeks to do the "Getting Ready" section. It will not work to jump into "Week Three" before first completing "Getting Ready." Feel free to revise the suggested format below in any way you think best.

Week 1

1. Have each man write his name, address, phone number, and email address on page 7 of his copy of *The Making of a Dangerous Man.*

2. Have each man take 2-3 minutes, beginning with you, to share what motivated him to be part of this "Dangerous Man" group. After expressing his motivation, have each one share his address, phone number (home and/ or cell), wife's name (if married), and names and ages of his children. Have each man record the information on the "Men on My Team" sheets.

3. Take turns reading through "There's Danger Ahead," each man reading several paragraphs. Make sure you communicate that it is fine to say,

"I pass," if any of the men feel uncomfortable reading aloud. If desired, after each one reads a few paragraphs, allow time to interact over what was read.

4. Interact over the question, "What do you think are the greatest dangers a man faces?"

5. Take turns reading through the "Getting Ready" section until you reach the "Circle Exercise," each man reading several paragraphs. If desired, after each man reads, allow time to interact over what was read.

6. Clarify the assignment to be done before your next meeting:

   - Do the "Circle" and "Square Exercises."

   - Read the "As You Begin..." in the "Getting Ready" section and answer the questions.

   - Read and reflect over the rest of the "Getting Ready" section: "The Most Horrible Thing That Could Happen," "What Benefits Can You Expect?," and "What Is Expected of You?"

7. Allow 5-10 minutes to split the group in twos and threes and have each man share one thing which he would appreciate prayer for and pray for each other.

Week 2

1. Split up in pairs for 5-10 minutes to interact over the results of doing the "Circle" and "Square Exercises" during the week.

2. As a large group, give each man the opportunity to pick two or three questions that caught his attention under the "As You Begin..." section and share how they assessed themselves. They can also share why that particular question caught their attention.

3. Turn to the "Game Plan for Week Three" and have a volunteer read "The Challenge" and "The Goal."

4. Take a minute for each man to think about and identify his best time and place for his appointment with God during the coming week. Go around and give each man the opportunity to share the time and place that works best for him.

5. Clarify the assignment to be done before your next meeting:

   - During the following week, spend 10-15 minutes daily to do "Week One, Days 1-6." During your appointment with God, write your responses to the questions under "Respond" and "Your Story."

   - Be ready to share from one day's reading/appointment with God during your next meeting. Share from the day's reading/appointment with God what meant the most to you.

6. Optional: If time allows, do Week One, Day 1 "A Man's Career and His Identity" together as a group.

- Take turns reading "A Story of a Dangerous Man" about Ken Ruettgers.
- Read John 1:9-13.
- Give time for the men to respond to the questions under "Respond." Encourage the men to write their responses to the questions as they interact.
- Split into twos and threes for the men to respond to the questions under "Your Story."

7. Allow 5-10 minutes to split up in twos or threes to pray for each other that their appointments with God this coming week would be meaningful and for anything else desired.

Weeks 3-8

Interact over the following questions—give each man the opportunity to respond:

1. Is it working for you this past week to make space in your life to connect with your Heavenly Father in a real way for 10-15 minutes a day, or most days? If not, what changes do you need to make?

2. What story most impressed you?

3. What passage of Scripture most impressed you?

4. For you, what was the week's "take-away"—the one most important truth God impressed on you or one action step for you to take.

5. Was there a time during the past week when God impressed you with saying or doing something, but responding would have taken you out of your comfort zone? How did you respond?

Allow 5-10 minutes at the end of each session to split up in twos and threes to share one thing for which they would appreciate prayer and to pray for each other. Use the "Prayer Journal" pages to write down each other's requests. From time to time refer to Dawson Trotman's quote on page 130 to challenge each other to trust God and claim His promises in prayer.

Feel free to adjust the above format as God leads you to fit your group. Give space for men to share what they are learning in relation to the "curriculum of life circumstances" they are experiencing now.

Week 8

1. At the end of this session, take a couple minutes to look ahead at Week 9. This could be a very significant week for each man in doing *The Making of a Dangerous Man*!

2. Clarify assignment to be done before your next meeting:

   • Read "The Most Dangerous Man Who Ever Lived."

   • Respond to the questions you responded to as you began *The Making of a Dangerous Man*.

   • Respond to the questions in the section "A Few Evaluative Questions to Identify Changes and Growth."

Warning—don't try to rush the above. Allow sufficient time to use the questions as a springboard to confirm areas of growth and changes that you have been experiencing with God the past weeks. **Anticipate a dynamite time alone with God as you do this!**

Week 9

1. This week's exercise gives each one the opportunity to "nail down" the most significant things God has been doing in his life over the past weeks. Interact over each of the "A Few Evaluative Questions to Identify Changes and Growth." Each of these questions is significant. Allow sufficient time for each man to respond to each question. If more time is needed, plan to give another week to allow each man time to share and interact over his discoveries.

2. To prepare for Week 10, read together by taking turns "Your Story" on pages 126. Week 10 is a major transition in helping a man gain a clearer grasp of the story God has been writing in his life. The major vehicle to this perspective is the guidance of the Holy Spirit as a man identifies his unique turning points and impact on his life using the chart on page 127.

Week 10

1. Give each man the opportunity to share the turning points and the resulting impact on their life. After each man shares, give him the time to share his "Key Learnings" from identifying his turning points and their impact.

2. You may need to allow more than one week for each man to have sufficient time to share their turning points, impact on their lives, and key learnings from this exercise.

3. A strategic help to each man will be clarifying and interacting over the life area they would like to focus on to cooperate with God in specific ways. If the men share a common life area on which to focus, such as discipling one's children, they may want to continue to meet to help each other be intentional and specific.

Note: Giving each man the opportunity to share his story will better enable them to connect in a significant way.

Men on My Team

Name

Address

Phone   E-mail

Family

Name

Address

Phone   E-mail

Family

Name

Address

Phone   E-mail

Family

Men on My Team

Name

Address

Phone   E-mail

Family

Name

Address

Phone   E-mail

Family

Name

Address

Phone   E-mail

Family

Men on My Team

Name

Address

Phone   E-mail

Family

Name

Address

Phone   E-mail

Family

Name

Address

Phone   E-mail

Family

Frequently Asked Questions

"Do I Do *The Making of a Dangerous Man* Alone or With Other Men?"

You can do *The Making of a Dangerous Man* either by yourself or with other men. If you have circumstances in your life that prevent you from utilizing this tool with other men, by all means consider using this as a devotional tool alone for ten weeks.

If there is any way you could do this with one to three (or more) men, I would urge you to go for it.

Why? One significant reason: accountability. And if you don't like the sound of that word, how about "strong, mutual encouragement."

Left to ourselves, we often quit too soon. But if there is someone else who knows you and cares, and asks you, "How is it going? Are you making the progress you want to make?"—That can make the difference between quitting and keeping on. There is a real synergy that comes from connecting with someone of like heart.

Several years ago, my daughter Rachel said, "Dad, I know you've always wanted to run a marathon. If you still want to, I'll come and run the Twin Cities Marathon with you."

I thought to myself, "Yep, I really do want to run a marathon. It would stretch me, but I really want to do this." So I enthusiastically and hopefully took Rachel up on her offer. She was so committed to running this race with me that she promptly bought her plane ticket to fly from Colorado to Minneapolis. So now I had to run the race!

Let me tell you how the next nine months of training went:

It was a breeze. I planned out my training schedule, and I just followed my plan. No sweat! It went just as I planned with no hitches.

I'd better tell you before going any further that the above paragraph is a blatant lie!

If Rachel had not bought her plane ticket, I would have quit. I experienced colds, muscle sprains, hot, humid weather, and times when I really didn't feel like continuing.

During this time, I had frequent talks with Rachel on the phone about our training runs, rode my bike with my wife Shirlee on long training runs each Saturday, and ran a 15-mile training run with my neighbor Ed. They were the ones who made the difference between my quitting and keeping on.

And we did it! We both ran the marathon! Okay, I didn't put too much pressure on the front-runners, and I didn't set any records. But we finished the run and I was able to fulfill a desire I had had for many years. It was Rachel and her buying the plane ticket that made the difference!

How about you–what desires have been lying dormant in the recesses of your heart these past years? You have tried by yourself to fulfill those desires but seem to fall short of fruition. Isn't it time to ask a friend, or friends to join you and do *The Making of a Dangerous Man* together? Who could you "go for it" together with?

What Is the Ideal Number of Men to Do
The Making of a Dangerous Man With?

Greg Ogden, in his book *Transforming Discipleship*, tells how he made a startling discovery. He had written a discipleship curriculum that turned into the final project for his doctor of ministry degree. The focus of his project was to implement this curriculum in a local church and then to evaluate its effectiveness. Up to this time, he had equated making disciples with a one-to-one relationship.

His advisor wisely suggested he consider a variety of relational contexts in which he could test the curriculum and then track the dynamics of the discipling relationships. One of the options he chose was to invite two other men to join him. He has since come to call this a triad.[1]

Guess what he discovered: Without question, the setting where he experienced the greatest transformation in the lives of believers was a group of three men.[2]

"The Sweet Spot" of Transformation of a Man's Heart

If you are a golfer, you know your golf club has a "sweet spot." When you hit the ball in the club's sweet spot, you can feel it. And you anticipate a good, long drive. If you play baseball or softball, you know when you hit the ball in the sweet spot of the bat—the ball seems to jump off the bat with power and zing.

Greg discovered a powerful principle with three dimensions:

When we (1) open our hearts in transparent trust to each other (2) around the truth of God's Word (3) in the spirit of mutual accountability, we step into the Holy Spirit's sweet spot. This is where the Holy Spirit can access our hearts in a life-transforming way.[3]

So, what are the implications of this principle? Does it mean one shouldn't meet with a group of more than three men?

Not necessarily. Many men have found similar dynamics when a group of four men meet. If you are meeting with a larger group of men, you would do well to consider dividing into groups of three to four men for a major part of your time. Meeting with the same three to four men rather than with different men from week to week will build an environment of safety and trust.

Meeting in threes and fours enables men to experience "peer" discipling. It's not just one man discipling the others, but mutual discipling, where each man disciples the others.

Why a Format With Stories of Dangerous Men?

Does a format with stories of men highlight and glorify them and unduly make them Christian celebrities? You may be thinking that such a format is off-base, and you prefer to hear God speak to you directly from the Bible or your own experience. You do not want to be dependent on others for your spiritual nourishment.

So why a format that includes stories of men?

The Holy Spirit directed Paul to write some relevant thoughts:

"For whatever was written in former days were written for our instruction, that through endurance and through the encouragement of the Scriptures we might have hope." –Romans 15:4, ESV

Have you noticed how much of the Bible includes the stories of men? Men like Abraham, Noah, Moses, Joseph, Daniel, Job, Jeremiah, David, Paul, and Peter. God says His intent is for our instruction, encouragement and endurance, and that we might have hope. God is a God of hope who doesn't want us to quit through discouragement and losing hope. So the Holy Spirit moves the writers of Scripture to record these stories for our benefit.

I can't help but conclude that He does not want the stories of His gracious working in our forefathers' lives to be lost due to poor memories or neglecting to pass them on to the next generation. As I read Exodus, Numbers, and Deuteronomy, I recognize that God's constant refrain is, "Don't forget how I have been working on your behalf in the past years. Don't forget!"

C.S. Lewis recorded his thoughts on the different ways God works in our lives:

"He works on us in all sorts of ways. But above all, He works on us through each other. Men are mirrors, or 'carriers' of Christ to other men. Usually it is those who know Him that bring Him to others. That is why the Church, the whole body of Christians showing Him to one another, is so important. The Church exists for no other purpose but to draw men into Christ, to make them little Christs."[1]

As I have researched the stories of men for this book, I have noticed a common thread among them—God loves to use the stories of His working in one person's life to encourage another person. God used Edward Kimball to impact Dwight Moody, Louis Zamperini to impact Bob Boardman, and William Borden to impact Ken Taylor (author of *Living Bible Paraphrase*).

What is there that is so powerful about hearing about God's working in another man's life in a powerful way? Have you noticed that often these stories involve an extreme need that brings a man to the end of his human resources? Like Abraham receiving a promise of having a son at the age of 75 with his elderly wife. Almost laughable! And then being asked to sacrifice your only son—can there be anything more difficult?

But God in His mercy somehow comes through and meets person after person at their point of greatest need. And somehow God uses their stories of His grace and mercy to encourage our weakened, hope-starved hearts.

Jesus was asked by his disciples in Matthew 13:11, *"Why do you tell stories?"* He responded: *"...I tell stories to create readiness, to nudge the people toward receptive insight."* Stories were a vehicle to create readiness to hear God's message for them.

The Stories Our Children Most Need to Hear

In the book of Psalm, we are told of God's desire and design for the next generation in our lives:

"One generation shall commend your works to another." (verse 4) "They shall speak of the glory of your kingdom and tell of your power, to make known to the children of man your mighty deeds..." (verses 11-12)
−Psalm 145:4, 11-12, ESV

So the question comes back to us—how have we really experienced God and His adequacy and grace in the midst of our real life experiences? If we can see the story He has been writing in our life that integrates His purposes and design, we can then pass them on to our children and grandchildren. Then when they are at their "crunch" time, (the time when they will decide to follow either Christ or the enticement of a peer), they will have something to hang on to make a good decision—rather than finding a vacuum.

This is part of the value of "Week Ten's" challenge—to identify the turning points of our life and God's design and impact on our life through those turning points.

How many times have you, when faced with a significant decision or turning point in your life, recalled, "What would my dad say or think in such a time as this?" Guess what your children may think to themselves when they are faced with their own significant decision or turning point!

Vin Staniforth was born in England. While honeymooning in the United States, Vin was called home after his father became very ill. His father died two days after Vin's return. At that time he realized how much he still wanted to learn about and from, his father. He had sufficient opportunity to ask his dad questions he always wanted to ask, but never did.

It was the regret of not finding out more about him when he had the chance that moved him to write the book *Questions for My Father.*[2]

You can be confident that your children want and need to hear your story of how you have and are experiencing God's power and grace.

*"Read up on what happened before you were born,
dig into the past, understand your roots.
Ask your parents what it was like before you were born,
ask the old-ones, they'll tell you a thing or two."*
−Deuteronomy 32:7, The Message

NOTES

THERE'S DANGER AHEAD!

1. Jerry White, *Dangers Men Face* (Colorado Springs, NavPress), 13.

GETTING READY

1. John Eldredge, *Wild at Heart* (Nashville; Thomas Nelson Publishers, 2001), 87.

2. Ibid, 83.

3. Ibid, 161.

4. Ron Martoia, *Morph! The Texture of Leadership for Tomorrow's Church* (Loveland, CO; Group Publishing, 2003), 11.

5. Joe Erhmann & Brian Buffini, *How to Love and be Loved* CD series, Buffini & Company.

6. Ibid.

7. Walter A. Henrichsen, *Disciples are Made—Not Born* (Victor Books, 1974), 18.

WEEK THREE

Game Plan

1. Reader's Digest, October, 2005, *"Big Boys Don't Cry"* by Dianne Hales. 105.

Day One

1. HBO's "Real Sports with Bryant Gumbel," January 24, 2005.

Day Two

1. Parade Sunday Newspaper Magazine, *"He Turns Boys Into Men"* by Jeffrey Marx, August 29, 2004.

2. Ibid.

3. Neil T. Anderson, *Living Free in Christ* (Ventura, CA: Regal Books, 1943), 23.

Day Three

1. Joyce Brown, *Courageous Christians* (Chicago; Moody Press, 2000), 17-18.

Day Four

1. Chris Havel, *Green Bay Press Gazette*, PackersNews.Com, December 27, 2004.

Day Five

1. Joyce Brown, *Courageous Christians* (Chicago; Moody Press, 2000), 29.

2. Leighton Ford, *The Power of Story* (Colorado Springs; NavPress Publishing Group, 1994), 82-83.

Day Six

1. Neil T. Anderson, *Living Free in Christ* (Ventura, CA: Regal Books, 1943), 9-11.

WEEK FOUR

Day One

1. Joyce Brown, *Courageous Christians* (Chicago; Moody Press, 2000), 121-122.

Day Two

1. Joyce Brown, *Courageous Christians* (Chicago; Moody Press, 2000), 63-64.

Day Four

1. Dennis Byrd, *Rise and Walk* (New York: Harper Collins, 1993), cover, 228.

Day Five

1. W. Terry Whalin, *John Perkins* (Grand Rapids; Zondervan Publishing House, 1996), 25.

2. Ibid., 29.

3. Ibid., 66-67.

4. Ibid., 72.

5. Ibid., 105.

Day Six

1. Brennan Manning, *The Rabbi's Heartbeat* Colorado Springs; NavPress), 21).

2. Ibid., 36-37.

WEEK FIVE

Day One

1. Joyce Brown, *Courageous Christians* Chicago; Moody Press, 2000), 48-49.

Day Two

1. www.DiscipleshipCounselingMinistries.org, *My Journey.*

2. Neil T. Anderson, *Living Free in Christ* (Ventura, CA: Regal Books, 1993), 7, cover.

Day Three

1. John Piper, CD *How to Fight for Joy.*

Day Four

1. Dietrich Bonhoeffer, *The Cost of Discipleship* (New York: The Macmillan Company), 15, 21.

2. Bill Hull, at National Coalition of Men's Ministries Leadership Meeting, November 7, 2005, Denver, Colorado.

3. Dietrich Bonhoeffer, *Letters and Papers from Prison,* (Great Britain, 1953), cover.

4. Bill Hull, at National Coalition of Men's Ministries Leadership Meeting, November 7, 2005, Denver, Colorado.

5. Dietrich Bonhoeffer, *Letters and Papers from Prison,* (Great Britain, 1953), 173.

Day Five

1. Joyce Brown, *Courageous Christians* (Chicago; Moody Press, 2000), 51-52.

Reflection On The Week

1. J.I. Packer, *Knowing God I* (Downers Grove, Illinois; InterVarsity Press), 181.

2. J.I. Packer, *Knowing God I* (Downers Grove, Illinois; InterVarsity Press), 195.

3. J.I. Packer, *Knowing God I* (Downers Grove, Illinois; InterVarsity Press), 207.

WEEKS 6-8

GETTING READY

1. John Eldredge, *Wild at Heart* (Nashville; Thomas Nelson Publishers, 2001), 87.

2. Philip Yancey, *The Jesus I Never New* (New York; Walker and Company), 20.

WEEK SIX

Day One

1. Don Bartlette, "Macaroni at Midnight," from a Focus on the Family broadcast, 1983.

Day Two

1. Jerry White, *Dangers Men Face* (Colorado Springs, NavPress), 48.

2. Ibid., 48.

Day Three

1. Henri J.M. Nouwen, *In the Name of Jesus* (New York, Crossroad Publishing Co.), 10-11.

2. Ibid., 11.

3. Ibid., 16.

4. Ibid., 17.

5. Ibid., 25.

Day Four

1. Robert Boardman, *Unforgettable Men in Unforgettable Times* (Washington, WinePress Publishing, 211-213.

Day Five

1. Ibid., 23-25.

2. Ibid., 213.

Day Six

1. Paul Borthwick, *Six Dangerous Questions* (Illinois, InterVarsity Press), 97-99.

WEEK SEVEN

Game Plan

1. Paul Borthwick, *Six Dangerous Questions* (Illinois, InterVarsity Press), 98.

Day One

1. Betty Lee Skinner, *Daws* (Michigan, Zondervan Publishing House), 378.

2. Robert D. Foster, *The Navigator* (Colorado, NavPress), 1-2.

3. Ibid, 3.

4. Ibid, 4.

5. *The Navigators Daily Walk Devotional Sampler*, 21.

Day Two

1. Roy Robertson, *Developing a Heart for Mission; Five Missionary Heroes* (Singapore, Nav Media), 14-15.

Day Four

1. Jan Hetting, *Follow Me* (Colorado, NavPress), 101-105.

Day Five

1. Jim Downing, *Meditation* (Colorado, Dawson Media), 6-7.

Day Six

1. A. W. Tozer, *The Pursuit of God* (Pennsylvania, Christian Publications, Inc.), 24.

2. Ibid., 26.

3. Ibid., 30.

4. Ibid., 41.

Week Eight

Game Plan

1. David Murrow, *Why Men Hate Church* (Tennessee, Thomas Nelson Publishers), 1-2.

2. Scott Morton, *Down to Earth Discipling* (Colorado Springs, NavPress), 9.

3. Ibid., 10.

Day One

1. Ibid., 11.

Day Two

1. Joyce Brown, *Courageous Christians* (Chicago; Moody Press, 2000), 91-92.

Day Three

1. *Monte Unger, He Died Looking Me Straight in The Eyes*, LeRoy Eims, internet.

Day Four

1. Portions reprinted from *Daily Bread*, December 31, 1988, and *The Yale Standard*, Fall 1970 edition.

2. Ibid.

3. Ibid.

Day Five

1. Jim Petersen, *Evangelism as a Lifestyle* (Colorado Springs, NavPress), 7.

2. Jim Petersen, *Living Proof* (Tennessee, Christian Business Men's Committee), 7.

3. Jim Petersen, *The Insider* (Colorado Springs, NavPress), 25.

Day Six

1. QuotationsPage.com and Michael Moncur.

2. Scott Morton, *Down to Earth Discipling* (Colorado Springs, NavPress), 19.

Week Ten

1. Tom Paterson, *Living the Life You Were Meant to Live* (Nashville, Thomas Nelson, Inc.).

Prayer Journal

1. Robert Foster, *The Navigator* (Colorado Springs, NavPress), 26.

FREQUENTLY ASKED QUESTIONS

1. Greg Ogden, *Transforming Disciples* (Downers Grove, Ill.: InterVarsity Press, 2003), 9.

2. Ibid., 153.

3. Ibid., 154.

4. C.S. Lewis, *Quotable Christian Quotes* by Michael L. Cook, http://cnonline.net-The CookieJar/Quotes-Christian.html.

5. Vincent Staniforth, *Questions for My Father* (Hillsboro, Oregon: Beyond Words Publishing, Inc., 1998), cover.

To Order Additional Copies of

"The Making of a Dangerous Man"

Visit our website at:

www.dangerousman.org